ANDY MCILREE

Boaz

Ruth's Bridegroom, Redeemer and Lord of the Harvest

HAYES
PRESS Christian Publisher

First edition

This book was professionally typeset on Reedsy.
Find out more at reedsy.com

Contents

1

INTRODUCTION

The story of Ruth has found an honoured place in literature, but, right at the outset, we salute its much more highly prized place in Scripture. The romance of literature can stand on its own, needing neither background nor foreground, and most authors would derive satisfaction if their particular book gained recognition for its individuality. The Bible is never like that. The revelation of Scripture is completely different. Unlike literature's independence, the interdependence of all scriptural content reveals that background and foreground are essential to each individual part, and that Divine authorship is satisfied by its overall harmony. Ruth's contribution beautifully reflects this. In fact, if we miss the wonder of its wider application, we miss its true relevance. The events of the book are like a jewelled cameo woven into the fabric of Israel's chequered background. The account of Ruth's arrival on the pages of God's Word is an interweaving of His grace, His call – so typical of His reaching out to Abraham, Rahab, and to Gentiles – and His purpose. So, during Israel's dull days, she is like a colourful butterfly emerging from a very drab chrysalis.

There is no shallow end to the story of Ruth, as depths of despair at the beginning lead on to deepening delight, which causes us to exclaim, "*Oh, the depth of the riches both of the wisdom and knowledge of God! How unsearchable are His judgments and His ways past finding out!*"[1] Her story is a revelation, yet the inscrutable wisdom of God allows certain details to remain hidden. When it was written, where, and by whom, fade into the unknown, but why it was written brings each enquiring reader closer to what may be more fully known of God. The stunning reality is that He had the record penned when, generations later, prophecy had become history, and the One to whom both are the same had the man after His own heart[2] reigning in Jerusalem.

Mr Newberry dates the Judges from 1425 – 1120BC and sets Ruth at 1322 – 1312BC, which would place her story around the time of Shamgar and Deborah. Others place it during the rule of Gideon, suggesting that the conditions mentioned in Judges 6:1-6 coincide with those referred to in the first chapter of Ruth. Whatever may be the timing of the story's historic setting, the genealogy at the end of chapter 4 indicates that the earliest the book could have been written was in David's lifetime.[3]

Merely tracing the beauty of each gripping chapter is not enough for it soon becomes evident that a higher hand lies behind the tragedy and unfolding triumph. It is the hand of Omnipotence, which Naomi claimed had gone out against her,[4] and from which she would receive so much blessing. It's the story of two great journeys: one, from Bethlehem to Moab; the other, from Moab to Bethlehem; the first, from faith to faithlessness; the second, from faithlessness to faith; one, away from God by hearts that were wayward; the other, toward God by hearts that were won. Irrespective of away or toward, believer or unbeliever, of belief or unbelief, spiritual direction always begins in the heart.

The tragedy of the first journey for three – Elimelech, Mahlon and

Chilion – started and finished in the first five verses of chapter 1; the triumph for another three – Naomi, Ruth and Boaz – began in chapter 1 and lasted almost to the end of chapter 4. The final two verses crown the story of Boaz the redeemer and Ruth the redeemed, and anticipate the greater crowning of David, the king of Israel, through whom would come One whose crowning was greatest of all: Christ – God's King, and ours!

If we were looking at Abraham and Isaac's journey to Moriah in Genesis 22, apart from absorbing the actual event, we would see it as a foreshadowing of the Lord Jesus Christ's death at Calvary. In a similar way, the Spirit of God helps us to look beyond many Old Testament narratives to see their New Testament fulfilment, and there's outstanding value in doing this with the Book of Ruth. As we trace redemption's story in Ruth, the glorious light of the epistle to the Romans shines into the cameo and its foreshadowing follows its beam the whole way forward to the gospel of Christ.

Naomi and her family were characteristic of Israel as a nation, and their departure is symbolic of Israel's waywardness and unbelief. In Romans 9:1-5, Paul refers to their rejection of Christ and confesses: "*I tell the truth in Christ, I am not lying, my conscience also bearing me witness in the Holy Spirit, I have great sorrow and continual grief in my heart. For I could wish that I myself were accursed from Christ for my brethren, my countrymen according to the flesh, who are Israelites, to whom pertain the adoption, the glory, the covenants, the giving of the law, the service of God, and the promises; of whom are the fathers and from whom, according to the flesh, Christ came, who is over all, the eternally blessed God. Amen.*"

Having made known his longing for them, and his mourning, he moved on in chapter 11:12 to give the outcome of their hardening: "*Now if their fall is the riches of the world, and their failure riches for the Gentiles, how much more their fulness."* Through Israel's fall, salvation has come to the Gentile, and Paul's message for them in verses 30 and 31 is, *"For as you once were disobedient to God, yet have now obtained mercy through their disobedience, even so these also have now been disobedient, that through the mercy shown you they also may obtain mercy."* At present, God is being glorified as many Jews come personally to Christ for salvation and follow the host who turned to Him both at and after Pentecost in Acts 2. They are what God calls, *"a remnant according to the election of grace"* in Romans 11:5.

Another day is coming, when the time of great tribulation is over and the Lord Jesus Christ appears to win them nationally, as Romans 11:26, 27 promises: *'And so all Israel will be saved, as it is written: "The Deliverer will come out of Zion, and He will turn away ungodliness from Jacob; for this is My covenant with them, when I take away their sins."'*[5] God also promised in Jeremiah 23:8 to gather *"the descendants of the house of Israel from the north country and from all the countries where I had driven them. And they shall dwell in their own land."*

> Then from the east, and from the north,
> From every clime and strand,
> I have resolved to bring them forth,
> Back to the glorious land.

We can summarise a parallel of Ruth and Romans as follows:

- Elimelech and family leave Bethlehem - Their fall (Rom.11:25);
- Naomi returns, the only one of four - A remnant will return (Rom.9:27);
- Ruth reached by disobedient Jews - Gentiles reached after Jews'

disobedience (Rom.11:30);

- Ruth obtains grace and mercy - Gentiles receive mercy (Rom.11:30);
- Ruth obtains redemption - Gentiles receive grace through redemption (Rom.3:24);
- Naomi blessed through Ruth - Jews' fulness, after God's riches to the Gentiles (Rom.11:12).

In the sovereignty of God, Ruth came to God, His people and His land, because a Jewish family had become estranged, and this is the teaching we find in Romans chapter 11 as Gentiles are brought to Christ because of an estranged Jewish nation. In His infinite wisdom, God has made it that we have been blessed through the Jew, since *"salvation is of the Jews,"*[6] and they will be blessed through the Gentiles. This is summed up in the final verse of Hebrews 11 – *"God having provided something better for us, that they should not be made perfect apart from us."* Bearing all this in mind, we will learn from the ways in which these four chapters fit into the purpose of divine inspiration. None of us should ever read it without seeing how *"profitable"* it is *"for teaching,"* that its ups and downs are good for *"reproof"* and *"correction,"* and that its spiritual triumph is designed to give us *"training in righteousness."* Paul emphasised these aims in 2 Timothy 3:16 and 17 (ESV) with the intention that *"the man of God may be competent, equipped for every good work."* Our prayer is that Ruth's journey to Boaz, and with Boaz, will provide each of these in our own journey to Christ and with Christ.

Nine characters will take up our attention:

- Elimelech (husband) - 'God is my King';
- Naomi (his wife) - 'pleasant, sweet';
- Mahlon and Chilion (their two sons) - 'sickly, weak' and 'pining, failing';

- Ruth (Mahlon's widow) - 'friend, companion';
- Orpah (Chilion's widow) - 'the nape of the neck' - from '*araph*: to bend down) - a practising unbeliever refusing to go forward;
- Boaz (a close relative) - 'In whom is strength';
- The closer relative (probably Elimelech's brother) - a non-practising believer refusing to go forward;
- Obed (Boaz and Ruth's son) - 'Servant'.

Ruth always follows the book of Judges in western Bibles, but the Jewish Scriptures, the Tanakh, have a different arrangement:

- The Torah (The Law): Genesis, Exodus, Leviticus, Numbers, Deuteronomy.
- The Nevi'im (The Prophets): Joshua, Judges, 1 Samuel, 2 Samuel, 1 Kings, 2 Kings, Isaiah, Jeremiah, Ezekiel, Hosea, Joel, Amos, Obadiah, Jonah, Micah, Nahum, Habakkuk, Zephaniah, Haggai, Zechariah, Malachi.
- The Kethuvim (The Writings) - Psalms, Proverbs, Job, The Song of Songs, Ruth, Lamentations, Ecclesiastes, Esther, Daniel, Ezra, Nehemiah, 1 Chronicles, 2 Chronicles.

From the Kethuvim, five readings of the shorter scrolls called Megilloth are still reserved for certain festivals, and Ruth is elevated to a special place:

1. The Song of Songs – on the Feast of the Passover;
2. Ruth – on the Feast of Pentecost: Shavuot – the Feast of Weeks;
3. Lamentations - on the Fast of the ninth of Av (commemoration of the destruction of the Temple);
4. Ecclesiastes – on the Feast of Tabernacles;
5. Esther – on the Feast of Purim.

The story of Ruth stands in marvellous contrast to the book of Judges, which has just closed with the words, *"In those days there was no king in Israel; everyone did what was right in his own eyes."* The word *"right"* was normally a complimentary description, but its proper connotation of uprightness was lost when applied to their ungodly hearts and minds. In their case, it simply meant that they did what was convenient and self-pleasing, and that their twisted and crooked reasoning allowed them to think they were going straight. These were days in which Israel's relationship with God was inconsistent, as they rose to great heights and fell to great depths. Some of their leaders were like spiritual giants through whom He brought tremendous victories, yet the effects wore off and the people returned to their backsliding ways.

It's one of the wonders in the insect world that *"The locusts have no king,"*[7] but there was nothing commendable about the way in which God's people voiced their thoughts of a kingdom. What defiance they showed when they said to Samuel, *"No, but we will have a king over us,"*[8] and more so when they said to Pilate, *"We have no king but Caesar."*[9] These hostile expressions leave us in no doubt that the beginning and end of Israel's monarchy was marred by anarchy. History shows that mediocrity can so quickly descend into hostility in any generation, but these words together with defeat should never belong to the Christian's vocabulary, since Christ is the victor and victory is assured.[10] Ruth clearly demonstrates that: even in the darkest times when His people's testimony was at a low ebb, God was on the march, in His gracious sovereignty, doing *"whatever He pleases."*[11]

How significant it is, that the ultimate peak in Ruth's great story lifts our thoughts to David and not Saul, Israel's first king. This is significant in two ways: firstly, she was brought into the line of Judah of whom the prophetic word was, *"The sceptre shall not depart from Judah, nor the ruler's staff from between his feet, until Shiloh come; and unto him shall the obedience of the peoples be."*[12] Saul was from the tribe of Benjamin, and therefore didn't belong to the kingly line that God had chosen for His Son to come. The second was that giving Saul as king was in response to the people's impatient demand of which God said, *"I gave you a king in My anger, and took him away in My wrath."*[13] His eye was on the final word of Ruth's story – *"David"* – long before He called her into the mainstream of His purpose and, looking via the victor of Elah,[14] whom He declared the *"man after My own heart,"*[15] He saw the One who was *"born of the seed of David"*[16]: *"Son of David"* – guaranteed the throne – and *"Son of Abraham"* – guaranteed the cross.[17] The nation lived like Job's friends, speaking unrighteously for God,[18] but God often stepped in, just as the Lord did to rectify Peter's misuse of his sword!

In his delightful book, 'Ruth the Moabitess', Henry Moorhouse speaks of lessons we can learn from Old Testament pictures and suggests the following:

* A Jew's going into a far country in chapter 1 is like the parable of the lost son in Luke 15.

* A Gentile girl's being brought into the land of blessing and marrying Boaz by means of a Jew's backsliding is a picture of Christ obtaining a bride.

* After their marriage, the Jewess (Naomi) was blessed again, which points to God's New Testament dealings with Israel: they backslide, Gentiles are blessed, the church is united to Christ, and then the Jews are blessed again.

God has woven the wonderful theme of the bride throughout the Old

Testament. For example:

- Adam and Eve − a bride through blood: prior to The Fall and sinless;
- Isaac and Rebekah − a bride through the Spirit: after Moriah and substitution;
- Ruth − a bride for the lord of the harvest and redeemer;
- The Song of Songs − a bride for the shepherd-king.

By combining this sequence, we have a wonderful glimpse into the glorious means by which God will obtain a bride for His Son: by no lesser route than through the blood of His cross, shed for fallen sinners, and the gracious ingathering work of His Holy Spirit. One by one, like Ruth, we come as Gentile strangers from our ungodliness in a far-off place to meet our Redeemer, the Lord of the Harvest. In the purpose of God she was brought into the kingly line, and so have we[19]; and like the bride in the Song of Songs with her bridegroom, we rejoice in our bridal relationship with the good Shepherd and King of kings.

The harvest fields of Judah certainly stand in marked contrast to the battlefields of Judges, and we discover that God's giants can be found among those who followed reapers as well as among those who led warriors. By grace, we see a glorious parallel to Psalm 24:7,8 where we read, *"Lift up your heads, O you gates! And be lifted up, you everlasting doors! And the king of glory shall come in. Who is this King of glory? The LORD strong and mighty, the LORD mighty in battle."* The same glorious Person, as God manifested in the flesh[20], was the speaker who said in John 4:35, *"lift up your eyes and look at the fields, for they are already white unto harvest."* So His victory is twofold: He is King of the battlefield and Lord of the harvest field.

As we begin to absorb the overall wonder captured in four short, dramatic chapters, we acknowledge that its inspiration declares the mind of the Inspirer, its laws project the heart of the Lawgiver, and its prophetic purpose shows the power of the Sovereign. We also will see ourselves reflected in discoveries the Moabitess made because of the lovely man, Boaz, and, as we consider his many resemblances to Christ, we will lift our eyes to that lovelier Man and worship the God of all grace.

The Way of the Cross

Some of us stay at the Cross,
Some of us wait at the tomb,
Quickened, raised, seated with Christ
Yet lingering still in the gloom.

Some of us bide at the Passover Feast
With Pentecost all unknown:
The triumphs of grace in the heavenly place
That our Lord has made our own.

If Christ who had died had stopped at the Cross,
His work had been incomplete.
If Christ who was buried had stayed in the tomb,
He had only known defeat.

But the Way of the Cross never stops at the Cross,
And the way of the tomb leads on
To victorious Grace in the heavenly place,
Where the Risen Lord has gone.
(*Annie Johnson Flint*)

2

THE TIMING

"Now it came to pass, in the days when the judges ruled ..." (Ruth 1:1)

* * *

Only four books in the New King James Version of the Old Testament begin with the words, *"Now it came to pass"* – Ruth, 2 Samuel, Esther and Ezekiel – and each of them, in its own way, indicates that it's not the biblical equivalent of saying, "Once upon a time." The first time that God used the little word *"yᵉhiy,"* from which the phrase comes, is found in Genesis 1:3 where we read, "Let there be," "and there was," and on that occasion He changed darkness to light. In a very different sense, the same could be said about the opening phrase of these four books: Ruth was brought from the spiritual darkness of Moab into the light of God's grace[1]; Saul's death would herald the light of His greatness being made known through David as king[2]; Esther would be used along with her cousin, Mordecai, for the light of His goodness[3] to shine into the darkness of Haman's intended persecution of the Jews; and Ezekiel was the means of the brightness of God's glory[4] being made known to His people in the darkness of their captivity in Babylon. Such great events have never been forgotten.

Ruth

To this day, the little book of Ruth is brought to the forefront by being read in the Jews' annual feast of Shavuot, which believers in the Lord Jesus Christ know as Pentecost. She is well remembered as the Gentile whom God drew as a foreigner to marry a wealthy Jew, so it's appropriate that the annual celebration of Shavuot should be a voice to Jews of God's desire to spread the message of the cross to other nations and draw Gentiles to Christ through the gospel.

David

In current Jewish practice, "The Book of Psalms is divided into five parts, parallel to the Five Books of Moses. It is further subdivided into seven parts, one for each day in the week, and further divided into 30 divisions, for each day of the month. Many Jews make it a habit to say a portion of the Psalms every day after the morning prayers, thus completing all the Psalms in the course of a week or a month." (From The Complete Story of Shavuot).

Another example is found each year on Yom Kippur, the Day of Atonement, when Psalms are recited throughout the day. The Jerusalem Talmud, *Hagigah* 2.3, says: "David died on Atzeret [Feast of Weeks]." According to Jewish tradition, this means that he was also born on that day, "Therefore one reads the book of Ruth, in order to honour David on his birthday" (Rabbi Shlomo Yosef Zevin cites *Tevu'ot Shor* on Baba Batra 13b).

Of much more spiritual value and importance are the verses in David's psalms that were fulfilled while the Lord was on the cross[5]:

- *"My God, My God, why have You forsaken Me?"*
- *"They divide My garments among them, and for My clothing they cast lots."*
- *"Into Your hand I commit my spirit."*
- *"He guards all his bones; not one of them is broken."*

Quotations fulfilled in the Saviour's crucifixion were succeeded by Peter's quotes from Psalm 16:8-11 and Psalm 110:1 in his message on the Day of Pentecost.[6]

* *"I have set the Lord always before me; because He is at my right hand I shall not be moved. Therefore my heart is glad, and my glory rejoices; my flesh also will rest in hope. For You will not leave my soul in Sheol, nor will You allow Your Holy One to see corruption. You will show me the path of life; in Your presence is fullness of joy; at Your right hand are pleasures forevermore."*

* *The LORD said to my Lord, "Sit at My right hand, till I make Your enemies Your footstool."*

Esther

* The book of Esther is read every year at their feast of Purim and, in contrast to Ruth, she was a Jewess who married a wealthy Gentile.

13

Ezekiel

* The people of Israel's return from Babylon is well documented in the books of Ezra and Nehemiah.

When the Judges Ruled

Divine order is vital among God's people, and He had already made this known in the appointment of Moses as mediator and Aaron as high priest. It's interesting that these were two brothers of the same father and that, together, they pointed forward to the only Son who is One with His Father. In the perfect will of God, His Son is the fulfilment of both. He is the Apostle, prefigured by Moses who stood before the people for God; and He is the High Priest, portrayed by Aaron who stood before God for the people.[7] In Moses' case, his father-in-law indicated that he was insufficient for the job and advocated his need of assistance.

With this in mind, he assured Moses, *"The thing you do is not good. Both you and these people who are with you will surely wear yourselves out. For this thing is too much for you; you are not able to perform it by yourself."*[8] This resulted in Moses choosing *"able men, such as fear God, men of truth."*[9] There's no doubt that these were men of ability, sanctity and integrity, but it's not clear whether God had initiated their selection or if it was only Jethro's considered opinion. He certainly invoked the name of God three times when he said, *"Listen now to my voice; I will give you counsel, and God will be with you: stand before God for the people, so that you may bring the difficulties to God."*

Whatever the rights or wrongs of accepting Gentile advice, we can be absolutely sure of one thing: the Lord Jesus Christ is uniquely able and needs none to help him as *"Mediator of the new covenant."*[10] Nor does He need others to assist Him as great High Priest for, as such, *"He is also able to save to the uttermost those who come to God through Him, since He always lives to make intercession for them."*[11] He is eternally adequate as Mediator *"by means of death"* – no other ever died to save lost sinners, therefore none can help; and He is eternally adequate as High Priest, since no other *"ever liveth"* (RV).

After the death of Moses, his role was passed to Joshua (*Y^ehōshuwa*, meaning Jehovah saves), and Aaron's *"garments of ministry"*[12] were passed on to Eleazar, which means God is Helper. What a lovely Christlike combination! We could hardly miss noticing that the book of Joshua closes by referring to three burials – Joshua, Joseph and Eleazar – and how the triumphant testimony of these three godly men buried at home in the Promised Land allows the book of Judges to open against its faithful background. How different, then, that the book of Ruth should open with three burials – Elimelech, Mahlon and Chilion – and we note the tragic testimony of three men buried among ungodly men, far from home in the unfaithful background of a foreign land.

The time of the judges presents a line of saviours who pre-dated the appointment of a king. Within this orderly arrangement, God had a wonderful way of ensuring that, where He gives triumph, there will be a testimony to what His people have experienced. Rahab heard a detailed account of how they crossed the Red sea on dry land and of subsequent God-given victories.[13] Others heard, too. Whole nations heard. No wonder the people rejoiced as they sang, *"The people will hear and be afraid ... The mighty men of Moab, trembling will take hold of them; All the inhabitants of Canaan will melt away. Fear and dread will fall on them."*[14] Long before Ruth was born, her people were disturbed by what they had heard, and there was more to come in the days of the judges.

What a variety of characters they were, yet we see glimpses of Christ in the meaning of many of their names.

- Othniel - "the force of God" - (1 Cor.1:24; 2 Cor.13:4)
- Ehud the Benjamite - "son of the right hand, united" (Ps.80:17)
- Shamgar - "the cup-bearer" (Matt.26:27; 1 Cor.11:25)
- Gideon - "the feller" (Heb 2:14; 1 Jn 3:8)
- Tola - "the scarlet worm" (Ps.22:6)
- Jair - "the enlightener" (Jn 1:4,5; 8:12; Eph.1:18)
- Jephthah - "he will open"(Lk.24:31,32,45; Acts 16:14)
- Samson - "the sunlight" (Mal.4:2; Rev.1:16)

Ruth may have heard of Israel's historic achievements, but it's unlikely she hadn't known about how Ehud ended Moab's eighteen years of rule over Israel by killing its king, Eglon, with a two-edged sword. Once again, it would be etched in the Moabite mind that their mighty men were no match for the mighty God. Just as He had depicted in Moses and Aaron glories that would be available in His Son, so we trace features of Christ in the judges He had chosen.

How could we fail to see that Jesus is our Othniel, 'the force of God' revealed as *"Christ the power of God"*? He is our Ehud, who although a Benjamite – a son of the right hand – is described as *"left-handed,"* which implies his right hand was maimed or bound. Our Saviour is the Man of God's right hand, yet He came as if manhood had limited Him. But, no: just as Ehud, in apparent weakness, overcame his adversary with a two-edged sword, so also the One who was crucified in weakness overcame our adversary. In His humanity, He was God manifested in the flesh, still the Son of the right hand and unlimited in power. Being made in our likeness never made Him more vulnerable or less victorious for He *"shared in the same, that through death He might destroy him who had the power of death, that is, the devil."*[15]

He is our Gideon, and we can say to Him, "You are our feller." Even in His defencelessness and lowliness, as the One who said, *"But I am a worm, and no man,"* He is our Tola; and He is our Jair through whom the eyes of our heart are enlightened. Our hearts were closed to Him, yet He alone is their opener. Perhaps, right now, it will be good for each of us to pause, just to check if from a more personal point of view we are truly able to say, 'Jesus, You are my opener. You are my force of God, my Son of the right hand, my cup-bearer, my feller, my scarlet worm, my enlightener, and my sunlight.' He is mightier than Samson, and much brighter, for God *"has shone in our hearts to give the light of the knowledge of the glory of God in the face of Jesus Christ."* These and other judges were God-given deliverers, yet His people slumped from deliverance to defeat as they came and went. They were overcome until their saviour overcame, and so were we until our Saviour came to prove that He was waiting to deliver us.

> Two glad services are ours,
> Both the Master loves to bless.
> First we serve with all our powers –
> Then with all our feebleness.
>
> Nothing else the soul uplifts,
> Save to serve Him night and day,
> Serve Him when He gives His gifts –
> Serve Him when He takes away.
> *(C.A. Fox)*

The day also is coming when, *"He who scattered Israel will gather him, and keep him as a shepherd does his flock. For the Lord has redeemed*

Jacob, and ransomed him from the hand of one stronger than he. Therefore they shall come and sing in the height of Zion, streaming to the goodness of the Lord."[16] From days much darker than were known in Moab, the redeemed of Israel will be brought back to God as the fullest answer to Naomi's homecoming to Bethlehem and to Him. All twelve tribes will come like tributaries of a river merged into one, and they will flow more spontaneously than ever was known in days when they went up to Jerusalem for the feasts of Jehovah.

As the word *w^{e}nāh^{a}rū* implies, they will be sparkling like a river with the glow of sunlight on its surface for the goodness of the LORD, their Redeemer, will be shining on them as He sees them drawing near and acknowledges that they are not appearing before Him empty-handed[17] or empty-hearted.

They used to sing the Songs of Ascents, songs of the going up composed of Psalms 120 to 134, as they journeyed, and as they neared Jerusalem they would hear the welcoming sound of the Temple singers, but this time they will meet the Singer of Hebrews 2:12 and hear the welcome of their Saviour.

Careless seems the great Avenger; history's pages but record
One death-grapple in the darkness 'twixt old systems and the Word;
Truth forever on the scaffold, wrong forever on the throne —
Yet that scaffold sways the future, and, behind the dim unknown,
Standeth God within the shadow, keeping watch above His own.
(James Russell Lowell)

3

THE DECISION

"Now it came to pass, in the days when the judges ruled, that there was a famine in the land" (Ruth 1:1).

* * *

God's promised response to order and disorder was embedded in His law: He blessed the former and judged the latter. It is clearly set out in Leviticus 26, and excerpts from verse 3 to 20 show how clear-cut His conditions were:

"If you walk in My statutes and keep My commandments, and perform them, then I will give you rain in its season, the land shall yield its produce ... Your threshing floor shall last till the time of vintage, and the vintage shall last till the time of sowing; you shall eat your bread to the full ... You will chase your enemies, and they shall fall by the sword before you ... You shall eat the old harvest, and clear out the old because of the new ... I will walk among you and be your God ... But if you do not obey Me ... you shall sow your seed in vain ... for your land shall not yield its produce ..."

This was fulness at its best. There would be such abundance that bringing in last year's crop would keep them busy until next year's sowing. Feeding from the past harvest would have a surplus rather than a shortage, and their storehouses would need to be emptied to make room for the incoming crop. God's earlier promise of unceasing *"seedtime and harvest"*[1] was wonderfully harnessed to His later assurance of grain from the threshing floor and wine from the vintage, which coupled promised feeding with promised joy. His abundant supply meant that hands and hearts should be full, not only for themselves, but for Him. In return for His rich blessing, a tenth of their produce was given to the Levites to sustain them in their priestly service and they, in turn, offered a tenth of that as a heave offering to God.

As they did this, His response was, *"And your heave offering shall be reckoned to you as though it were the grain of the threshing floor and as the fulness of the winepress."*[2] This meant that, out of their fulness of joy, He received fulness of joy, and so the cycle of blessing was complete: they were blessed by His giving, and He was blessed by theirs. It was like an Old Testament example of New Testament believers being able to say, *"Blessed be the God and Father of our Lord Jesus Christ, who has blessed us."*[3]

The people of Israel were triply blessed in the ways God provided for their needs. In Exodus 15:26, He took care of their sickness by saying, *"I will put none of the diseases on you."* In Leviticus 26:7, He took care of their security by assuring them, *"You will chase your enemies."* And in Isaiah 1:19, He added to His earlier promises of plentiful harvests by taking care of their satisfaction by saying, *"If you are willing and obedient, you shall eat the good of the land."* How then could couples like Elimelech and Naomi be confronted with conditions that prompted their decision to go elsewhere?

Famine in the Land

There should be no lack in God's land. It should be renowned for its fulness and fruitfulness. Oh, if only His churches were well known for the richness of their feeding. Is your assembly like that? God wanted His land to be a place of storehouses, and it's essential that His house takes character from that. Every assembly should have the spiritual wherewithal to keep its storehouse amply filled, and there's something far wrong if His Word is in short supply.

This brings us to consider the sad statement that He made through Amos: "'Behold, the days are coming,' says the LORD God, 'that I will send a famine on the land, not a famine of bread, nor a thirst for water, but of hearing the words of the LORD. They shall wander from sea to sea, and from north to east; they shall run to and fro, seeking the word of the LORD, but shall not find it.'"[4] May God keep us from ever experiencing a famine for "hearing" His Word, from times when either personally or collectively there is no hunger to hear it or for the impact of having it expounded. This is the worst of all famine. It's one thing to deprive the stomach, quite another to starve the soul. Amos was urged to "Go ... Flee to the land of Judah. There eat bread, and there prophesy. But never again prophesy at Bethel."[5]

No bread in Bethlehem, the House of Bread; and no word from God in Bethel, the house of God. If they had been asked why they didn't want to hear from Amos, they may have said that they never got anything out of it, and that would have revealed more about the hearer than the speaker. Our prayer meetings should be times of pleading that God will never stop speaking through His servants, that they always will have something from Him to say; and our teaching meetings should be times of hearing what He has to say. We should graciously encourage one another that there be no shortage of speakers and no shortage of hearers.

> Master, speak; Thy servant heareth,
> Waiting for Thy gracious word,
> Longing for Thy voice that cheereth;
> Master, let it now be heard.
> I am listening, Lord, for Thee –
> What hast thou to say to me?
> (F.R. Havergal)

We need the spirit of Elisha who, in a time of acknowledged dearth, immediately told his servant, *"Put on the large pot, and boil stew for the sons of the prophets."*[6] His sense of trust in God made him see beyond the famine, not to a small pot, but to a great one; and not to a cold meal or a reheat, but to something freshly cooked and hot. This holds a valuable lesson for any like the Scottish minister who was criticised for giving "Caul kail het again," meaning he repeated an old sermon, like reheated food. Elisha's story is covered in four verses, during which his intended meal became deadly, yet he was equal to this, too, and provided the remedy by calling, *"Then bring some flour."*

The New King James Version translates the next phrase rather tamely: *"And he put it into the pot,"* but this fails to convey the urgency of his action. Other versions say he "cast" it in, and some say that he "threw it," and they capture the meaning of the word *wayyashlēk*. The urgency of his calling, when Elijah *"threw his mantle on him"*[7] – he didn't 'put it on him' – went on to become the urgency of his service, and we see this when he *"cast in the salt"* to heal the bitter water[8] and *"cut off a stick, and threw it in"* to retrieve the sunken axe head.[9]

May God help us to be equal to the task in our day. Thank God for men like Elisha who face up to reality and take the initiative to do something about it! As a man of God, he would have been well aware why there was a famine in the land, and for that reason he acted by faith. But what happens when there are no Elishas? Perhaps, we can glimpse an answer in the opening verses of Jeremiah 14 by wondering at the nobles' lack of reality. A few questions will be enough to tell us what sort of men they were.

* Had they completely overlooked the fact that dearth and drought were signs of God's disapproval? Had they forgotten His warning? – *"'I will give you the rain for your land in its season, the early rain and the latter rain, that you may gather in your grain, your new wine, and your oil. And I will send grass in your fields for your livestock, that you may eat and be filled.' Take heed to yourselves, lest your heart be deceived, and you turn aside and serve other gods and worship them, lest the Lord's anger be aroused against you, and He shut up the heavens so that there be no rain, and the land yield no produce, and you perish quickly from the good land which the Lord is giving you."*[10]

* Could they not read His displeasure on their parched land?

* Did they fail to see that no rain, no grain and no grass meant that He had withheld them?

They were supposed to be the excellent, yet they failed to show that, *"As for the saints who are on the earth, 'They are the excellent ones, in whom is all my delight.'"*[11]

It wasn't the first time that nobles had failed for Nehemiah 3:5 speaks of those who shared in the effort of rebuilding the wall, *"but their nobles did not put their shoulders to the work of their LORD."*

* Was it beneath their dignity? And was it for the same reason that their successors *"sent their lads for water,"* to spare their blushes? Did they think they were above getting their hands dirty, and beneath them to have their hearts cleansed?

* Why send lads when the futility was so obvious? Young people, even in our day, may have their weaknesses, but the onus is never on young people when there's no refreshing feeding among the people of God. Leaders must lead, and feeders must feed!

Israel's mercurial state in the time of the judges made the downside of Leviticus 26 a reality. The people ceased walking with God and He stopped walking with them. They had disregarded His order and gone beyond the boundary of His promise: *"If you walk ... I will walk,"* so blessing changed to judgment. Famine ravaged the land, not only Bethlehem itself, yet being there depicted the poverty of the nation by emphasising famine in the House of Bread. God had taken the *Lechem* out of *Bēth Lechem.* Bethlehem is referred to as *"Bethlehem, Judah"* in verse 1, which distinguishes it from the other Bethlehem in the territory of Zebulun[12] and the family are described as *"Ephrathites of Bethlehem"* in verse 2.

This attributes fruitfulness to the place, but they would never be able to say, like Joseph, *"God has caused me to be fruitful [pārāh, linked to Ephrathah] in the land of my affliction."*[13] Truest fruitfulness came to Bethlehem when the Saviour was born there, of which Micah says, *"But you, Bethlehem Ephrathah, though you are little among the thousands of Judah, yet out of you shall come forth to Me the One to be Ruler in Israel, Whose goings forth are from of old, from everlasting."*[14]

Militarily and agriculturally, God was the means of their protection and production, and everything was governed by this one rule, "If you walk ... I will walk." But notice the change in His wording in these verses: He began by referring to "the land" and ended by calling it "your land." The Lord Jesus Christ made a similar change when He referred to the Temple in Jerusalem as "My house" and as "Your house."[15] How tragic it is when there is no evidence of His presence or blessing and when what was His simply becomes ours! This was a real danger in places such as Ephesus and Laodicea[16] where those who had been called into churches that belonged to God risked being at the stage when they would merely speak of them as "our church." The land, first and foremost, was His, and those in the land must live as being His. The assemblies, first and foremost are His, and those in them must live as being His. Only then can we say, as in the words of Psalm 85:1 and 12, *"LORD, You have been favourable to Your land; ... Yes, the LORD will give what is good; And our land will yield its increase."* His first, then ours!

When we walk with the Lord
In the light of His Word,
What a glory He sheds on our way;
While we do His good will,
He abides with us still,
And with all who will trust and obey.

Then in fellowship sweet
We will sit at His feet,
Or we'll walk by His side in the way;
What He says we will do;
Where He sends, we will go,
Never fear, only trust and obey.
(John Henry Sammis)

25

Famine in the Heart

Others went through difficult times too. When King Saul *"inquired of the LORD, the LORD did not answer him, either by dreams or by Urim or by the prophets."* God was completely silent: no answer was given within himself, the high priest had nothing to say to him, nor did the prophets. The truth was, the LORD had departed from him,[17] and had stopped communicating with him. Had he possessed the spiritual sensitivity of his successor, David, he would have cried out to God, *"O LORD my Rock: Do not be silent to me, lest, if You are silent to me, I become like those who go down to the pit."*[18]

With the insensitivity that comes from famine in the heart, Saul took his problem elsewhere, and his solution was to disguise himself and go to consult a witch. What a ludicrous move for a man who was head and shoulders above everyone else! It wouldn't take a witch to see through his disguise, but it would seem she didn't. She was supposed to be able to see into the future, yet she couldn't see through a disguise!

When Samson caved in to Delilah's questions and his hair was shaved off, *"he did not know that the LORD had departed from him."*[19] The sad thing was, he didn't know the difference. He had given in to a temptress and ended up bald, blind, and captured by the Philistines. King Hezekiah was another from whom God withdrew, *"in order to test him, that He might know all that was in his heart."*[20] How sad it is when those who should know better don't realise that when God withdraws He withholds.

We were thinking a moment ago of the church in Ephesus in Revelation 2 that risked having its lampstand removed. Would those in it have known any difference if it had been, or would they just have gone on as normal? The church in Sardis had a name of having life, yet it was dead. If the lampstand had been removed from Ephesus, would they not also have had a name of having light? Jeremiah spoke about the heart being deceitful,[21] and famine in the heart will make it even more so. Our Bibles give ample proof in both Old and New Testaments that, individually and collectively, it's possible to live with pretence.

God wants us to be real about our relationship with Him and to know the reality of His relationship with us. We reach times of spiritual crises when we turn away from Him, and are at a very serious crossroads if He ever needs to turn away from us. Yes, there can be times when we lose the assurance of knowing He is there for us, and He might be testing us to see what is in our hearts. At that point, we need to show that we have a heart for Him, and for what is His. If repentance is needed, there will be no hesitation when there is no famine in the heart.

Famine in the Home

Now it was Elimelech's turn. The famine was national, so there was no solution north or south. They were testing times, and he failed the test. This was no overnight, spur of the moment reaction. If we could have eavesdropped at the door of their home, we may have heard the process of this family's discussion, decision and departure. They might well have said, "We can't cope with this any longer. We have had enough. Staying here would be pointless. Anywhere will be better than here. The boys agree. Let's go." All four "went." Yes, they walked away, but the implications given by different forms of the word *hālak* are more serious than that. They wandered from their true home and vanished from their place among God's people in the land like the cloud that disappears and vanishes in Job 7:9.

Two valuable lessons can be learned from this kind of procedure. When we feel it is bad 'here' where God has called us, we should remember that it is much worse 'there' where He is not honoured. Furthermore, family decisions do not excuse us from personal responsibility or free us from individual accountability to God.

The word *"dwell"* (Heb. *gūr*) is translated differently in Numbers 22:3 where we read, *"Moab was exceedingly afraid."* It also means to go in fear as a stranger, to turn aside from the road, or to shrink in fear, and may indicate that this family had serious reservations and were afraid of what lay ahead. They had every reason to be for they left *"Bethlehem"* - the house of bread, and *"Judah"* – the place of praise,[22] thanksgiving,[23] and confession,[24] and went to *"Moab"* which originated from the son of Lot after his incest with one of his daughters.[25]

Another interesting connotation from the word *gūr* is found in Psalm 33:8 where the psalmist says, "Let all the inhabitants of the world *stand in awe* of Him." Whatever could there be in Moab that would cause them to stand in awe other than with a sense of fear? They were turning their backs on Bethlehem and God's land where they could stand in awe of Him in true reverence, but there would be nothing to revere in Moab. When they "went," did they intend only to be visitors who would retrace their steps at the first opportunity? If so, they sound a loud warning to believers who assume that departure from God will be a temporary measure they can put right whenever they please. Ten years in Moab testify to how short-sighted faithlessness is for it proved to be a decade in which the absence of faith's long-sightedness deprived them of enjoying the Passover and engaging in the other feasts of Jehovah.[26] Three deaths show that permanence can easily be masked by temporary intentions, which fail to take into account that repentance can't be guaranteed or pre-arranged. There would be no shortage of sorrow for them in Moab, but it wasn't of the godly sort through which

God in His goodness grants repentance.[27] There would be tears over three coffins, and later at the crossroads when Orpah decided to give up the journey to Bethlehem and return to Moab, but not tears of contrition.

The famine in the land had triggered a famine in their hearts until it became a famine in the home for the whole family, and what a loud warning this is that dearth in the church can lead to dearth in our Christian homes! It can be the other way around, of course. Is it not true that our hearts and homes determine the state of the church? Our struggles affect us. Elimelech and Naomi's natural struggle became spiritual: faith decreased and fear increased. Had David been among their predecessors instead of their successors, they could have taken his advice, *"Trust in the LORD, and do good; dwell in the land, and feed on His faithfulness."*[28] They also could have taken the rebuke from Solomon had they been able to read, *"For the upright will dwell in the land, and the blameless will remain in it."*[29] It's a wonderful promise to many, and an indictment for others like Elimelech and family. They didn't "remain," so they couldn't claim to be "upright" or "blameless."

More than three thousand years have passed since then, but this doesn't reduce the need to ask, "As they prepared to leave and finally made their exit, did anyone urge them not to go?" Maybe they did: perhaps not. Either way, there's a lesson for us. Our love for the Lord, and for our brothers and sisters, should make us want to help some toward better decisions and to reassure them that God still says, *"If you walk … I will walk."*

Lord, Thou hast made Thyself to me
A living, bright reality,
More present to faith's vision keen
Than any earthly object seen;
More dear, more intimately nigh
Than e'en the closest earthly tie.

And Thou, blest vision of my soul,
Hast made my broken nature whole;
Hast purified my base desires,
And kindled passion's holiest fires;
My nature Thou hast lifted up,
And filled me with a glorious hope.

Nearer and dearer still to me,
Thou living, loving Saviour be;
Brighter the vision of Thy face,
More charming still Thy words of grace;
So, life shall be transformed to love,
Thy grace and mercy more to prove.
(Charlotte Elliott)

4

THE CONSEQUENCE

"*And a certain man of Bethlehem, Judah, went to dwell in the country of Moab, he and his wife and his two sons. The name of the man was Elimelech, the name of his wife was Naomi, and the names of his two sons were Mahlon and Chilion—Ephrathites of Bethlehem, Judah. And they went to the country of Moab and remained there.*

Then Elimelech, Naomi's husband, died; and she was left, and her two sons. Now they took wives of the women of Moab: the name of the one was Orpah, and the name of the other Ruth. And they dwelt there about ten years. Then both Mahlon and Chilion also died; so the woman survived her two sons and her husband" (Ruth 1:1-5).

* * *

Like it or not, decisions have consequences. We know that, don't we? It's as old as Eden. As individuals, Eve and Adam saw and thought, made their decisions, and ate. Their foreseen consequences should have included God's forewarning about eating of the tree of the knowledge of good and evil: *"in the day that you eat of it you shall surely die."*[1] Their unforeseen consequences meant they didn't even have the knowledge that they would attempt to hide out of sight of the Omniscient, and have lost the desire to be with Him. Both actions were an admission that His promise had been fulfilled: spiritually, they had died. We know, of course, that God went after them and that, even though they were removed from the Garden of God, He had a plan to bring man back into fellowship with Himself.

Elimelech and his family were like a re-run of this. Individually, they saw and thought, they made their decision, and acted. Were they blind to the foreseen and the unforeseen or was their consideration of these outweighed by a decision about bread? One thing is sure, the adversary didn't make truth and the God of truth a priority as he helped them to read his faulty scales, and the perceived imbalance made them decide to leave His land. Bread tipped the scales! Like Adam and Eve, this family were in it together, yet sin always has made man individually accountable to God.

They would have admitted that lack of bread was their reason for leaving, but they would have been more honest had they admitted that the real reason was lack of love. They were like the church in Revelation 2:4, and God could have said to all four of them, *"Nevertheless I have this against you, that you have left your first love."* Sadly, we never see things the way God sees them when we turn away from Him and His service. Other things get the blame, even other people, yet God knows that the underlying cause is in the heart, not the feet. Paul had been able to say of this church in Ephesus, *"I heard of your faith in the Lord Jesus and your love for all the saints,"* but this changed. The same probably could have been said of Elimelech and his family, but their outlook changed too, and apparently neither God nor the people of God were good reason to stay.

The consequences were hard-hitting: three men lost their lives, three wives lost their men, and one widow lost the joy of being a mother. How right Solomon was when he said, *"The way of the unfaithful* [plural participle of *bāgad*] *is hard."*[2] They were a snapshot of what God sometimes saw in His people: He *"made the tribes of Israel dwell in their tents. Yet they tested and provoked the Most High God, and did not keep His testimonies, but turned back and acted unfaithfully* [from *bāgad*] *like their fathers."*[3] However, just as Genesis 4 shows that God received something acceptable from Abel after the crisis of Eden, Ruth 1 opens up the wonderful foreshadowing of how He would gain something out of Elimelech and Naomi's loss. Not only would Naomi point to His bringing Israel back to Himself, but that Ruth would show his purpose in drawing Gentiles to the Redeemer.

Already, at the beginning of this chapter, there is a compelling lesson to be learned: if we are tempted to turn aside from our Christian path, we should be honest about what distracts us from God. For Adam and Eve, it was fruit; for Elimelech, Naomi and their sons, it was bread. What will it be for us? What is it for you? Whatever it was for them, look at it this way: was it worth losing fellowship with God over their one-off enjoyment of fruit? They certainly never tasted it again, so it was a fleeting and seeming gain followed by permanent loss. Was it worth losing fellowship with God and His people for bread? Three men were an Old Testament proof that, *"Man shall not live by bread alone."* They had that in Moab and died, but failed to live *"by every word that proceeds from the mouth of God."*[4]

What appeals to you that outweighs your relationship with God? A partner who doesn't know the Lord? A job that will make you give up your Christian principles? Or are you just attracted to the world and its worldly ways? Yes, you may be tempted to think that God could bring something good out of it, but the truth is that Adam and Eve didn't think of that before they forfeited the garden. Neither did Elimelech and his family before forfeiting the land, and neither should we before going our own way. Wrong decisions have the ability to delude, and consequences can be serious. In the case of the prodigal son, he came back to his father with a lot of regret, yet he soon discovered that eating the "fatted calf" was much better than "pods."⁵

God keep us from the prodigal's appetite. Luke 15:16 tells us that, *"he would gladly have filled his stomach with the pods that the swine ate,"* and that was tragic for a Jew. Pigs should have been farthest from his mind, and the law should have kept them off his diet, since it stated in Leviticus 11:7, *"the swine ... is unclean to you."* The problem was, he wasn't prepared to make the law personal and say, "the swine is unclean to me." Poor spiritual judgment can have an effect on the Christian's desires, too, and the world has its own way of catering to them. Many Christian lives have been damaged, and some ruined, by craving wrong things in wrong places with the wrong company. The truth is, it never runs out of "pods."

God is My King

When Elimelech was born his parents' choice of name probably voiced their own conviction and aspirations for him, that he would live up to its meaning – 'God is my King.' Each time they called his name they announced that God is Sovereign; more than that, they would have testified their desire that he would acknowledge God as Sovereign by submitting to His rule. The meaning of his name is quite significant, but the record of the book of Ruth shows that he didn't live up to it and lost his desire to be subject to Him. Like those who called Jesus "Lord, Lord" and failed to do what He asked, Elimelech answered to the name of "God is my King" without showing that He reigned as Monarch in his heart. He exchanged Canaan for Moab and went to live in different surroundings with its different gods where his God and King was not accepted as Sovereign.

The meaning of Elimelech's name combined with Naomi's – sweetness – sound like symptoms of an ideal spiritual relationship with God. Sweetness is sure to reign where God's sovereignty is acknowledged, but going to Moab was equally symptomatic that where there is no submission to Him sweetness will vanish, too. The names he and Naomi chose for their sons didn't reflect the godly ambition of his parents, and this may indicate a lower sense of God already existed in his way of thinking. David said, *"The LORD sat enthroned at the Flood, and the LORD sits as King forever,"*[6] but not in Elimelech's heart.

If only, like others, he had stayed in God's land without bread rather than in a land with bread but without God! Mahlon (from *chālāh*) implies thoughts of being sick, weak, diseased, infirmity, worn out, and wounded; and Isaiah alluded to the root meaning of his name when he spoke about the inhabitant of Jerusalem not saying, *"I am sick"* (from *ch°liy* and *chālāh*).[7] He had begun his prophecy by saying, *"The whole head is sick, the whole heart faints,"*[8] and Paul gave a New Testament counterpart when he wrote, *"many are weak and sickly among you, and many sleep."*[9]

Sadly, it wasn't long until Elimelech, together with his weak and sickly sons, also slept the sleep of death.[10] Chilion suggests wasting, pining, failure and destruction. Both names may refer to illness during infancy, but, whatever the reason, together with Elimelech's failure they combine to represent the poor spiritual condition of the people of Israel during the time of the judges. Isaiah also uses the thought of Chilion's name when he says to Israel, *"A remnant of them will return; the destruction [killāyōn] decreed shall overflow with righteousness."*[11] One commentator has written, "The word *killāyōn* from *kālāh* to complete, to finish, to waste away, vanish, disappear, denotes a languishing, or wasting away, as in disease; and then "destruction" or that which "completes" life and prosperity" (Albert Barnes). So Mahlon and Chilion's names, not only join to describe their poor physical health, but are combined by the Spirit of God to depict the people of Israel's poor spiritual health.

God is King

Elimelech's departure and demise teaches us that it's possible for "God is my King" no longer to be true, but one statement stands eternally true: "The LORD is King." With the waters of the Red Sea victoriously rolled over their enemies, the children of Israel concluded their song with the words, *"The LORD shall reign forever and ever."*[12] Around four centuries later, the psalmist wholeheartedly agreed: *"The LORD is King forever and ever."*[13] Difficult times may come and go, times may change, but He is unchangeable.

After hearing that five-year-old schoolchildren in his sister's class didn't believe in God, a four-year-old boy was asked what he thought about Him. He started off, "God is beautiful, and He made me." Suddenly remembering part of the answer to the fourth question in the Westminster Shorter Catechism, he added, "God is Spirit, infinite, eternal and unchangeable." How true! At the end of his Lamentations, Jeremiah wrote over what was a very dark time for God's people, *"You, O LORD, remain forever; Your throne from generation to generation."*[14] Yes,

He is enthroned in heaven from generation to generation, yet not every generation will show that He is enthroned on earth in their hearts.

She was left

What sad words! Naomi "was left" without her husband and in the burden of her widowhood it wasn't long until Mahlon and Chilion who had married Ruth and Orpah also died, and their deaths meant that, yet again, she "was left."[15] God always makes sure that something is "left," and Naomi is an example of His purpose in delivering a "remnant" of His people. Ezra spoke of it when he thought of those who returned from captivity in Babylon and attributed their escape to God's grace being shown to a "remnant."[16] Almost three centuries earlier, Isaiah had rested on the thought that *"the remnant who have escaped of the house of Judah shall again take root downward, and bear fruit upward."*[17] Naomi was of the house of Judah, and God was about to unfold how important her return would be.

As we shall see later, uppermost in the mind of God was the foreshadowing she gave of those from the people of Israel who respond to the call of the gospel of Christ and show that they are among the *"remnant according to the election of grace."*[18] He also looks forward to a coming day when *"The Redeemer will come to Zion, and to those who turn from transgression in Jacob."*[19] On that day, they will look on Him whom they pierced,[20] *"And he shall be their peace."*[21] He is the long-promised One of Bethlehem Ephrathah, *"The One to be Ruler in Israel, Whose goings forth are from of old, from everlasting"*; and then Micah adds, *"Therefore He shall give them up, until the time that she who is in labour has given birth; then the remnant of His brethren shall return to the children of Israel."*

Naomi's sons had married two Moabite women, Orpah and Ruth, and although Moab was not specifically mentioned in Deuteronomy 7:3, both Ezra and Nehemiah included Moab's women as being unsuitable wives for men among the people of God.[22] Forging wrong bonds in the place of bondage was an additional tie to Moab, marriage to their people meant marriage to the place, and they settled down to a future in Moab. Fear had gone, adjustments had been made, they no longer felt like strangers, and were at home in Moab until they died there. The *Targum* says, "And because they transgressed the decree of the word of the Lord, and joined affinity with strange people, therefore their days were cut off."

Staying in Moab for ten years was a mistake, but it is easy to make other mistakes after an initial error: like telling another lie to cover up the first one! The mistake of becoming unsettled in Bethlehem and leaving it led on to becoming settled in Moab and never leaving it. Straying was wrong, and staying was wrong. These young men squandered ten years – wasted years. It's a sober lesson, for it's one thing for us to use the world, but quite another for the world to use us. Another solemn lesson has to be learned: God can take us away from what we get in the world without asking our permission, but the world can never take what we get from God without our permission.

It's not possible to settle in Moab and be settled with God at the same time! Scripture gives us some clear examples. In Judges 3:14, *"the children of Israel served Eglon king of Moab eighteen years,"* until Ehud slew him and delivered them. In 2 Samuel 8:2, David *"... defeated Moab. Forcing them down to the ground ..."* In Psalm 60:8, God said, *"Moab is My washpot."* He saw it as being like a vessel for menial use, such as a slave washing his master's feet, and subdued before a conquering God. Jeremiah wrote, *"Moab is destroyed."*[23] To their shame, Elimelech, Mahlon and Chilion didn't defeat, destroy or conquer Moab. Instead,

Moab defeated, destroyed and conquered them! Moab meant different things to different people, but it was to David what it was to God – a place to be conquered. Spiritually, it's a lesson for us that either it will defeat us or we will defeat it. We can rejoice that David's greater Son has conquered sin and death for us, but we have to learn to conquer worldliness for ourselves. We will see this clearly in our next chapter when Orpah shows that although she was out of Moab, Moab wasn't out of her. It will be equally clear that although Ruth wasn't yet in Bethlehem, Bethlehem definitely was in her.

We don't know how they blended in, but they must have been rather conspicuous when they arrived there looking out of place as Jews among Moabites. They would have been seen to be different, almost as different as Achan if he had worn in Israel the Babylonian garment he stole at Jericho.[24] But they couldn't remain different and blend in at the same time. Something had to go, and no doubt they let go what was precious to God, and should have meant most to them.

Sometimes, Christians merge into worldly ways for the same reason: they lose the will to be different and leave their *"first love."*[25] Many years ago, on a dark night in South India, two of us went looking for a Christian family whose address we didn't know, except for the general area where we knew they lived. Hoping that someone local to the neighbourhood could help, we stopped in a dimly lit street to ask an Indian lady. At first, we drew a complete blank, until we told her that our friend's parents were active Christians. Suddenly, a light went on in her mind: "Oh, that will be the woman in the white sari!" And she told us exactly where we would find her and her family. She was remembered for being different, and so should we.

I Look Not Back

I look not back; God knows the fruitless efforts,
The wasted hours, the sinning, the regrets.
I leave them all with Him who blots the record,
And graciously forgives, and then forgets.

I look not forward; God sees all the future,
The road that, short or long, will lead me home,
And He will face with me its every trial,
And bear for me the burdens that may come.

I look not round me; then would fears assail me,
So wild the tumult of earth's restless seas,
So dark the world, so filled with woe and evil,
So vain the hope of comfort and of ease.

I look not inward; that would make me wretched;
For I have naught on which to stay my trust.
Nothing I see save failures and shortcomings,
And weak endeavours, crumbling into dust.

But I look up - into the face of Jesus,
For there my heart can rest, my fears are stilled;
And there is joy, and love, and light for darkness,
And perfect peace, and every hope fulfilled.
(Annie Johnson Flint)

5

RETURNING TO THE LAND

"Then she arose with her daughters-in-law that she might return from the country of Moab, for she had heard in the country of Moab that the LORD had visited His people by giving them bread. Therefore she went out from the place where she was, and her two daughters-in-law with her; and they went on the way to return to the land of Judah. And Naomi said to her two daughters-in-law, "Go, return each to her mother's house. The LORD deal kindly with you, as you have dealt with the dead and with me. The LORD grant that you may find rest, each in the house of her husband." So she kissed them, and they lifted up their voices and wept.

And they said to her, "Surely we will return with you to your people." But Naomi said, "Turn back, my daughters; why will you go with me? Are there still sons in my womb, that they may be your husbands? Turn back, my daughters, go—for I am too old to have a husband. If I should say I have hope, if I should have a husband tonight and should also bear sons would you wait for them till they were grown? Would you restrain yourselves from having husbands? No, my daughters; for it grieves me very much for your sakes that the hand of the LORD has gone out against me!"

Then they lifted up their voices and wept again; and Orpah kissed her mother-in-law, but Ruth clung to her. And she said, "Look, your sister-in-law has gone back to her people and to her gods; return after your sister-in-law." But Ruth said: "Entreat me not to leave you, or to turn back from following after you; for wherever you go, I will go; and wherever you lodge, I will lodge; your people shall be my people, and your God, my God. Where you die, I will die, and there will I be buried. The LORD do so to me, and more also, if anything but death parts you and me." When she saw that she was determined to go with her, she stopped speaking to her" (Ruth 1:6-18).

∗ ∗ ∗

With the weight of three deaths and three widows on her shoulders, Naomi must have wondered, "What should I do now? Where is God in all this? Where do I go from here?" Job knew that a meaningful part of his ministry was that he *"caused the widow's heart to sing for joy,"*[1] but who was there to make Naomi's heart sing? David's assurance in Psalm 68:5 wasn't available to her, yet the God of whom he spoke was always available as *"a defender of widows ... in His holy habitation."* Ruth and Naomi would find out how true this is after they reached Bethlehem, and, long before it was written in Psalm 146:9, each of them would prove that *"The LORD watches over the strangers; He relieves the fatherless and widow."* When news came that He had returned to bless His people, she knew what to do, and the comments are so informative: *"Then she arose ... for she had heard ...Therefore she went."*

Isn't it so typical of human nature that three deaths hadn't been enough to send Naomi back to Bethlehem, but the news of bread did? So the start of her journey back there was probably based on the wrong reason. It would have been much more meaningful if she had been prompted only by hearing the greater news *"that the LORD had visited His people,"* and not by hearing that *"the LORD had visited His people by giving them bread."* The next verse sums up her motive: *"Therefore she went out from the place where she was."* She left because there was no bread, and went back because there was bread. How sad! It's like going to church for help that's practical or social, rather than for what's spiritual! However, it did mean that His people's condition had changed: they were walking with God and providing the right spiritual climate for a new convert and a homecoming believer. The same is needed today. Churches should always be ready for the Lord to add those in whom He is working.

Naomi wasn't there when Jehovah came to bless – just like John 20:24 where *"Thomas ... one of the twelve, was not with them when Jesus came."* Even today, some dear Christians learn by hearsay what faithful saints learn by first-hand experience, because they ignore the warning, *"not forsaking the assembling of ourselves together, as is the manner of some."*[2] They not only miss the gatherings of the Lord's people, they miss out when He comes in blessing. However, a sovereign God has a sovereign purpose, which means there is a way back. Hard lessons can be learned from lean times, from departure and disappointment, and Naomi learned that, no matter how far you go or how long you stay away, He can provide the way back. The lure of the world might be like the decaying corpses that appealed to Noah's raven in Genesis 8:7, but Naomi's homing instinct kept her from finding true rest.

Some Christians find it even harder than she did for they are like doves that choose to fly with ravens! As Dr Andrew Bonar put it, "I look for the church and I find it in the world. I look for the world and I find it in the church." This leads us to draw a very distinct conclusion: Elimelech's failure wasn't due to another attack by Moab. It didn't result from outward conflict, but from inward collapse. Similarly, with churches today: on the whole, decline isn't caused by an increase in outward foes, but by a decrease in inward faith. In other words, it's not resulting from what we are facing, but on what we are turning our backs!

Following Naomi's response, it says of Orpah and Ruth, *"they went with her."* What a lovely phrase, and it conveys a bit more than simply going with each other. Like the word *"went"* in verse 1, they walked away and vanished together from Moab. But the picture of going *"with her"* brings them even closer for the word 'imāh comes from the word 'amam, which Dr Strong says can mean to overshadow by huddling together. We don't know how far they went until Naomi voiced what was troubling her.

Go, return ...Turn back ...Turn back

We can't know for certain why Naomi was so persistent. Perhaps, she didn't want to take the evidence of her wayward and costly ten years back to Bethlehem. Was she so ashamed? Was she testing them? Or was she an Old Testament example of trying to find out if someone was there only for the loaves and fish? How tragic it was that she should do her utmost to turn them back and drive them away from the way to Judah, the pathway to praise! This was discouragement wrapped in a kiss, desertion concealed by affection, and a deception that they could find the Lord's kindness, comfort and rest in the place where she couldn't. No wonder they *"wept"* (Heb. *bākāh*), lamenting and mourning at the very thought of parting. This was their personal *"valley of Baca,"*[3] induced by an Israelite and not a fellow-Moabite.

No doubt her kisses were sincere, but they masked the deeper reality that she was prepared to lose the only link with her boys, probably because she had lost her spiritual vigour. Ten years had drained her of faith's dependence and she had no vision of the possibilities of God for her daughters-in-law. Her kisses may have been warm, but her heart was cold. She was shaken in her faith, so couldn't help theirs! She may have thought they had built up hopes that would end up with raised expectations being dashed. Was that her reason for saying, *"If I should say I have hope"*?

Jews refer to their hope as their *'tiqvah'* – and Rahab, the stranger, visibly bound her *"scarlet cord"* (*tiqvah*) in the window. Yes, she had hope, a hope that brought her right into the heart of things to settle in Israel with a real sense of belonging. What she didn't know was that God had brought her into the mainstream of His purpose, as we find in Matthew 1:5 which says, *"Salmon begot Boaz by Rahab."* Elimelech and Naomi would have known this for she was able to say, *"This man is ... one of our close relatives."*[4] Rahab's hopes were more than fulfilled, and Ruth's would be too when this stranger met the earlier stranger's son!

Other possibilities are that she feared they were merely excited by the prospect of going to a foreign country to experience a different culture and customs, and thought they could regret it; or she wondered if they would be accepted among God's people and survive having their new religion tested in its homeland. She may even have been reflecting on how her family had left its inheritance and treated it so cheaply, and wondering if strangers would pay the price of commitment to God's service. Is it not also true in our case that those who prize their spiritual inheritance will encourage others to experience it too, while those who don't will fail to urge them on? Whatever her motive was, her three attempts to persuade them were attached to three different reasons.

1. The LORD would look after them (1:8);
2. There was no hope of future husbands (1:11-13) – limiting God;
3. They and their gods had no place among her people (1:15).

Having declined Naomi's first appeal, this time Orpah decided to go back and, with her kiss leaving its final imprint of fading affection, she disappeared over the horizon, out of their lives and from the pages of God's Word. Among the thoughts connected to Orpah's name, Dr Strong links it to the words 'oreph and 'āraph, which refer to "the back" and "to bend downward." At the turning point of her journey, it was as if she bent downward to write "Orpah" in the dirt with her back to Bethlehem and her face toward Moab. In doing so, she prefigured her nation's action in Jeremiah 48:39, *"How Moab has turned her back with shame!"*

Sadder still, God had already described Israel's response to Him in a similar way in Jeremiah 2:27 – *"For they have turned their back to Me, and not their face."* Saddest of all, we read in John 6:66 that *"many of His disciples went back and walked with Him no more."* We may find it hard to think of Orpah turning her back on Naomi, but how can we even begin to take it in that these men turned their back on the Saviour? They saw Him, they heard Him, yet, Orpah-like, they turned away from being in the presence of God manifested in the flesh. How could they have been so privileged, and decide to face the other way?

What we have to recognise, of course, is that we can see ourselves in Orpah and in these men, and it may be as you read this that the Lord is asking you, as he asked others in John 6:67, *"Do you also want to go away?"* Are you tempted to give up, because you are disappointed or disillusioned? Yes, it can happen, and it may be happening to you, but turning your back is not the answer. Much better to be like Jephthah in Judges 11:35 and say, *"I have given my word to the LORD, and I cannot go back on it."* By contrast, Ruth *"clung"* to Naomi with a bond that was first intended for married men who would *"be joined"* or *"cleave"* to their wives.[5] It is such a strong bond that Isaiah 41:7 translates it as *"soldering"* – fused and united as one.

Even so, Naomi remained determined and tried once more to dissuade Ruth: "Look, your sister-in-law has gone back to her people and to her gods; return after your sister-in-law." This must have been an unbearable thought for Ruth: back to the culture, customs and confusion of Moab among its people and their practices. It was unthinkable. Their main deity was Chemosh: *"the destroyer, subduer, or fish-god, the god of the Moabites (Num.21:29; Jer.48:7,13,46). The worship of this god, "the abomination of Moab," was introduced at Jerusalem by Solomon (1 Kin.11:7), but was abolished by Josiah (2 Kin.23:13)"* (Easton's Bible Dictionary).

Naomi's reasoning on the basis of Orpah's decision inferred that they would lack company and that there would be none of their own kind, but she overlooked the fact that anyone could feel at home among the people of God. Orpah had been encouraged to go back to idolatry by an Israelite, but when Naomi urged Ruth to "Look" she made it clear that her *look* was fixed in the opposite direction. Naomi had influenced her sister-in-law, but she would not influence her. Orpah couldn't resist the temptation to go back, and Ruth was irresistibly drawn to go forward! Thoughts of *"her mother's house"* and *"the house of her husband"* appealed to Orpah, but neither *Bēt 'immāh* nor *Bēt 'iyshāh* attracted Ruth. There was only one thought in her mind – *Bēt Lechem*, the house of bread.

Entreat me not to leave you

Orpah had shown the genuineness of her affection and the shallowness of her conviction, whereas the genuineness of Ruth's affection was sealed in the fulness of her conversion. Hers was a perfect surrender. There was more in her heart than a fondness for Naomi; it was set on the home of faith in the only true God and of love for Him and His laws.

She knew that going back would be taking away her inner sense of the call of God of which she had become so convicted, and she knew that going back would silence the voice of repentance that was burning in her heart. Turning to Naomi, she made an appeal that could come only from the heart of a woman in whom God was deeply at work. Evidence flowed from her as she spoke those momentous words:

"Entreat me not to leave you, or to turn back from following after you; for wherever you go, I will go; and wherever you lodge, I will lodge; your people shall be my people, and your God, my God. Where you die, I will die, and there will I be buried. The LORD do so to me, and more also, if anything but death parts you and me."

She had made a spiritual calculation and knew that going back would have meant a lost opportunity to enjoy:

- Direction – *"wherever you go, I will go;"*
- Communion – *"wherever you lodge, I will lodge;"*
- Union – *"your people shall be my people,"*
- Submission – *"and your God, my God."*
- Anticipation – *"Where you die, I will die, and there I will be buried."*

Submission held all five certainties together and, wisely, Naomi made no attempt to alter what she had said. What a lesson! When God is at work in a person's heart, there's no need to tell them what to say. There's nothing sweeter or more precious in evangelism than hearing the spontaneous prayer of a newly convicted sinner. Not all will be as eloquent as Ruth, no two will say the same, but the plea from genuine hearts, no matter how faltering, will complete the Spirit's work. It's the voice of repentance composed in the troubled sinner's own heart, not by a concerned believer. Ruth knew nothing about the road she was going or what her lodging place would be like; she knew very little about the people or what her burial place would be like; but she knew God and what He was like. In fact, her word for God is very revealing.

Twice she used the word Elohim, a plural name for the triune God, yet she never dreamt that He was calling her into the line that would lead to the incarnation of His Son. What she did see was that even death would not separate her from Naomi. She had the vision of being faithful unto death, and such was faith's grand anticipation that she grasped the reality of being gathered to her people, like Abraham, Isaac and Jacob,[6] Aaron and Moses,[7] Joshua[8] and David.[9] There is no mention of her ever kissing Naomi, but such words on her lips made a kiss redundant! She also confirmed her promise by calling on God to judge her if she ever went back on her word, which was an oath invoked by others in Israel.[10] Ittai also made a similar statement to David.[11]

Ruth's pledge shows that her allegiance to a person, a place, and a people had its higher focus on God. Take Him out of it, and she cannot say, *"your God, my God,"* and identifying with *"wherever you go ... wherever you lodge"* and *"where you die"* is completely futile. Naomi was to Ruth what Israel and the law are to the Christian. As far as Israel is concerned, "their fall is the riches of the world"; and we value the law as being the tutor that brought us to Christ.[12] Alas, Naomi in her disturbed state probably missed that her daughter-in-law had so eloquently echoed God's covenanting promise in Leviticus 26:12, *"I will walk among you and be your God, and you shall be My people."* Totally different from Orpah, Ruth knew how serious it was to make a pledge in His name and is an outstanding example to believers who make a commitment in baptism that they will not return to their old lifestyle or habits.

She had not the slightest idea of what the way would be like, she had very little idea of what the people would be like, and she had no idea whatsoever of what her life's content or her death would be like, but she put her hand into the hand of God knowing what He is like and that was all that mattered. There might be decline. That doesn't mean to say that you have to decline. There might be casualties round about you; that doesn't mean that you have to become one. Ruth stood at that moment of crisis and gave her firm commitment under the calling of God, inside the purpose of God, responding irresistibly to the grace of God. And she moved towards her objective – Bethlehem, even though she had never seen it before. She was determined.

Her determination registered with Naomi for *"When she saw that she was determined to go with her, she stopped speaking to her."* There is quite a contrast here. Ruth was *"determined"* (*hit'améts* – to stiffen one's self firmly upon a thing (Keil and Delitzsch Commentary on the Old Testament); and Naomi *"stopped speaking"* (*chādal* – to be flabby). What a difference! Ruth's resolve was strong, but there was no robust response from Naomi. Her reasoning was so weak that she was left with nothing to say. Speechless and silent, she had no words of thanks, of approval, or of praise to God. At this juncture of their journey, Ruth demonstrated that she had defeated Moab. It was destroyed and it had lost its appeal.

G. F. Dempster wrote a book called, 'Touched by a Loving Hand,' and this title could be written over the story of Ruth. There are particular words woven into it that we find a dozen times in chapter 1, once in chapter 2, and twice in chapter 4, and they all come from the little word *shūb*. In the course of chapter 1, it is translated as "return," "turn," and "gone back," all of which refer to Naomi and Orpah's intentions. In chapter 2:6, it refers to Ruth's volition in accompanying Naomi to Bethlehem. However, there's a major change in its use in chapter 1:21

where Naomi acknowledges that the LORD *"has brought me home again."* It was His work. What an admission, even though she felt "empty"!

Finally, we find it again in chapter 4:15, this time translated as "a restorer" for Naomi. Not only had God turned her back to Himself, He provided another to be the restorer that she could never be for herself. Is this not the best of all encouragement? There's never a right time to turn away from God, but it's always the right time to turn to Him or to turn back to Him. If you have turned away, let him bring you back, and you will be able to put the same word into your life and say with Psalm 23:3, *"He restores my soul."*

> Hast thou heard Him, seen Him, known Him?
> Is not thine a captured heart?
> Chief among ten thousand own Him,
> Joyful choose the better part.
>
> Idols once they won thee, charmed thee,
> Lovely things of time and sense;
> Gilded thus does sin disarm thee,
> Honeyed lest thou turn thee thence.
>
> What has stripped the seeming beauty
> From the idols of the earth?
> Not a sense of right or duty,
> But the sight of peerless worth.
>
> Not the crushing of those idols,
> With its bitter void and smart;
> But the beaming of His beauty,
> The unveiling of His heart.

'Tis the look that melted Peter,
'Tis the face that Stephen saw,
'Tis the heart that wept with Mary,
Can alone from idols draw:

Draw and win and fill completely,
Till the cup o'erflow the brim;
What have we to do with idols
Who have companied with Him?
(Miss Ora Rowan)

6

WALKING TOGETHER

"Now the two of them went until they came to Bethlehem. And it happened, when they had come to Bethlehem, that all the city was excited because of them; and the women said, "Is this Naomi?" But she said to them, "Do not call me Naomi; call me Mara, for the Almighty has dealt very bitterly with me. I went out full, and the LORD has brought me home again empty. Why do you call me Naomi, since the Lord has testified against me, and the Almighty has afflicted me?" So Naomi returned, and Ruth the Moabitess her daughter-in-law with her, who returned from the country of Moab. Now they came to Bethlehem at the beginning of barley harvest" (Ruth 1:19-22).

* * *

Bethlehem! They would have seen it as it appeared on the horizon, with differing thoughts being kindled in them as it gradually became nearer and clearer. Recognisable to Naomi, as she wrestled with mixed thoughts of leaving and arriving, it was unrecognisable to Ruth, as she rested in her thoughts of leaving Moab and forming first impressions of her new homeland. They were together in the House of Bread to be blessed in its fulness, and together among Ephrathites to be blessed in their fruitfulness. Chapter 1 opens with a family who took their eyes off God and left Bethlehem, and it ends with God setting His eyes on Naomi and bringing her back to Bethlehem. More than that, as Ruth's story portrays, He had His eyes fixed on a brighter horizon that Jew and Gentile would be called to discover in Christ.

Paul spoke well of Him in Romans 1:4 when he described Him as being *"of the seed of David according to the flesh, and declared* [Gr. *horisthentos* from *horizō*] *to be the Son of God with power."* Through the Saviour's incarnation, crucifixion and resurrection, God has "declared" or shown His Son to be the horizon of His purpose and, like Naomi and Ruth, He will draw both Jew and Gentile to Him. Through saving grace, they enter into the blessing of the bread of heaven in the true Bethlehemite, and into the greater fruitfulness of the true Ephrathite.[1]

All the city was excited

Ten years away from God and His people had taken their toll and, without knowing how harrowing these years had been, the womenfolk didn't hide their surprise and shock. They probably deduced by seeing two lonely women that Elimelech, Mahlon and Chilion were no more. One thing was certain, three-quarters of her family were missing. She hadn't come back the way she went, so it was understandable that there should be the noise of commotion and uproar after such a long separation. The New King James Version says they were "excited." We should love that word when it means a spiritual excitement in the service of God.

Perhaps, we have known similar times when a brother, sister or whole family has gone away from the Lord and sad experiences have left their mark. At that point, God entrusts them to the gatherings of His people for their spiritual needs to be understood, and met. It's a time for hearts to be moved as theirs were, and as the prodigal's father was in Luke 15:20 when he *"saw him and had compassion, and ran and fell on his neck and kissed him."* His feet followed the moving of his heart. He was a man who was triply moved: first of all, it was inward, then outward, and finally toward. Naomi was left in no doubt that these women felt for her. She saw their reaction, and wasn't put off by it. How important it is to react in the right way. Did she not sense a welcoming spirit? And was there not a meeting of hearts as she heard their question, and responded to it?

Is this Naomi?

Did the women ask their question because they were moved by how much her once recognisable features had been altered, and at her evident decline? "Is this Naomi?" They voiced their concern, as if to say, "Is it really you, Naomi?" By replying, *"Do not call me Naomi, call me Mara,"* she very pointedly asked them not to see sweetness in her, but bitterness. It was her way of acknowledging that the old identity had gone and had been replaced by a new name that reflected her years of estrangement. Remembering that she is an illustration of Israel as a nation, we can see that the question lingered more than seven hundred years later until Jeremiah asked in Lamentations 2:15, *"Is this the city that is called the perfection of beauty, the joy of the whole earth?"* And it resurfaced again when the Saviour came into that great city of Jerusalem and *"all the city was moved, saying, 'Who is this?'"*[2] The One who is *"great"*[3] was there and *"the city of the great King"*[4] didn't know Him! It was *"the city of our God"* and *"God was in her palaces"*; it was not only of God, He was in it, and the same should be true of churches of God. The people of Israel refused to own Him as God or acknowledge that His greatness is:

· infinite, because His deity is eternal and unsearchable;[5]
· ultimate, because He is incomparable;[6]
· intimate, because it is communicable.[7]

We have no such difficulty for He makes Himself known to us and continues to share His greatness with us through a deepening relationship with Him as *"our great God and Saviour Jesus Christ,"*[8] as *"great High Priest,"* and as the *"great Shepherd of the sheep."*[9] We can say, like Jeremiah, "His compassions fail not. They are new every morning; great is Your faithfulness."[10] He also gives *"songs in the night"*[11] and great comfort by helping believers to say, *"the night also is Yours."*[12]

the Almighty ... the LORD ... the LORD ... the Almighty

In response to their concerned openness with her, she referred twice to Jehovah and twice called Him Shaddai, while openly confessing all four as having a negative connotation for her. By renaming herself Mara, she testified that bitterness had replaced pleasantness: her sweetness and beauty had evaporated in Moab, but very graciously no one called her by her choice of name. Instead she was called by 'pleasantness' at least a dozen times in the remainder of the book, and we can be assured that this was of God, otherwise her sense of bitterness would have continued in Bethlehem. There were no negative reminders, and no raking up or casting up of the past. Repentance cleared the record, and personal bitterness didn't become communal!

Had anyone asked, "Naomi, did you come home with repentance?" she probably would have said, "Yes, definitely." This is what these verses are all about – a repentant woman who was searching her heart and, in the bitterness of her soul, trying to admit what was going on inside as she sought to become right with God and with His people. By calling her by her real name, it was as if she was being reminded, "Naomi, you are forgiven." As you read this, you may be looking back and wishing that certain things had never happened in your life, too. Friend, God says, "Are you repentant? You're forgiven and it is gone."

Individual bitterness

In a very personal way, Esau had his own 'Mara' experience when he heard that his father, Isaac, had blessed Jacob, and *"he cried with an exceedingly great and bitter cry."*[13] Once kindled, this bitterness quickly became deeply rooted in Esau and turned into hatred and murderous intent that took twenty years to resolve. He certainly proved that *"The heart knows its own bitterness,"*[14] and we need to fear the deadly effects of Mara experiences, especially when we feel justified in harbouring them.

Collective bitterness

Bitterness is self-destructive, and potentially of others too. If, individually, it has to be feared, collectively, its contagion has to be dreaded. The bitter water at Marah in Exodus 15:23 was the children of Israel's first test after they had crossed the Red Sea, and it showed what bitterness can do. Having sung with Moses in verse 1, they complained against him in verse 24, and his immediate response was to call on God for the answer. The urgent action of casting a tree ('*ets* – a stick, as in 2 Kings 6:6) into the water removed the danger and made it sweet. When David wrote, *"Behold, how good [tōb – "joyful" as in Ecclesiastes 7:14] and how pleasant [nā'īm] it is for brethren to dwell together in unity,"*[15] he was thinking of the pleasantness that belongs to Naomi's name.

Sadly, bitterness can rob God's people of their joy, and Moses gave a very pointed warning about this that was particularly relevant to Naomi: *"that there may not be among you man or woman or family or tribe, whose heart turns away today from the Lord our God, to go and serve the gods of these nations, and that there may not be among you a root bearing bitterness or wormwood."*[16] There is nothing to suggest that she and her family served other gods in Moab, but they had exchanged God's land for a land of gods. Moses' words are echoed in Hebrews 12:15 where the warning is applied to how one person's bitterness can contaminate the assembly: *"Looking carefully ... lest any root of bitterness springing up cause trouble, and by this many become defiled."* The good thing is, in Exodus the people didn't remain at Marah, they moved on to the refreshment of Elim. Naomi must learn to do the same, and so must we. God hadn't called her back for her to hold on to where she had been!

She had used the name of the LORD in her appeals to Orpah and Ruth in verses 8 and 9, and referred twice to Him as *"the Almighty"* and twice as *"the LORD"* when describing her trials. Instead of El Shaddai being strongly for her, she felt He had been strongly against her, and she spoke about His open hand (*yad*) being against her. She may have been blaming Him, but, in her own way, perhaps she was acknowledging His right to make *"the way of transgressors ... hard."*[17] Ruth's positive awareness of the LORD in verse 17, and Naomi's lack of response seems to indicate that He had withdrawn from her. Isaiah and Joel combined both names when they said, *"for the day of the LORD is at hand! It will come as destruction from the Almighty."*[18]

The psalmist added a third name when he wrote, '*He who dwells in the secret place of the Most High shall abide under the shadow of the Almighty. I will say of the LORD,"* He is my refuge and my fortress, my God [Elohim], in Him I will trust.*"'*[19] They knew Him as strong in chastening, but also in comforting; strong to destroy, but also to defend. Without realising it, Naomi needed a greater sense of God.

full ... empty

"I went out full, and the LORD has brought me home." If Naomi had stopped there, she would never have said a truer word, but she spoiled it by inferring, 'He poured me out, He has spoken against me, and He has broken me in pieces.' As far as she was concerned, He had witnessed against her wayward existence in Moab and punished her by turning her fullness to emptiness. She was right when she said, *"I went out."* At least she was honest and didn't try to claim that the Lord took her out and she went back. Going out was her doing; coming back was His! It was an admission of her condition before Him, of how she felt inside, so with repentance and godly sorrow she acknowledged the impact He had on her during those ten barren years. If only we would confess to the place that 'I' has in our troubles! She had gone out 'whole' and came back 'worthless.' But He had not simply brought her back, He had brought her *"home"* and that was the most important thing for her to recognise.

She knew she was home. Do we? Is your church really your home? It should be. Or does a sense of emptiness deprive you of your enjoyment of feeling at home in it? The One who said, *"none shall appear before Me empty"*[20] is able to fill *"empty pitchers"* with light[21] and *"empty vessels"* with oil.[22] Like Paul, we can say, *"I know how to be abased, and I know how to abound."*[23] One thing is certain, and we can learn this from Naomi, it is much better to go back empty to the full place than try to get full in the empty place!

they came to Bethlehem

There are many in the Scriptures who walked together. Among the earliest partnerships, Genesis 5:24 says, *"Enoch walked with God; and he was not, for God took him."* It gives the impression that one day they walked and just kept going. The Partner never changed, only the scenery! Abraham walked with Isaac to Moriah, like the Father and His Son going to Calvary, and all they knew was that they were going to wherever God wanted to take them. It was like a Calvary walk. Afterwards, Eliezer and Rebekah walked together as if being examples of our walking by the Spirit,[24] like a post-Pentecost and pre-Rapture walk. Other couplings include Joshua and Caleb, Ezra and Nehemiah, Joshua and Zerubbabel, Haggai and Zechariah, Paul and Barnabas, and the company of disciples whom the Saviour sent out *"two by two."*[25] All of them were coupled in a trustworthy fellowship with each other, and together with Him. A dear sister once told me that she had never had a close confidante, yet God often brings fellow-saints together for dependable confidentiality.

Naomi and Ruth were another of God's great couplings, and this was shown, not only by leaving Moab together, but in the timing of their arrival in Bethlehem for *"they came at the beginning of barley harvest."* Barley was the first crop to be reaped[26] and harvesting began immediately after the Passover, which was held on the 14th day of the month Abib (also called Nisan), and followed by the Feast of Firstfruits. The first was the great foreshadowing of the Saviour's suffering and death in the lamb; the second pointed forward to the joy of His resurrection in the wave sheaf. The chapter closes with a wonderful contrast to the way it opened. Returning replaces leaving, harvest replaces hunger, and the scene is set for a new beginning. It was as if God said to them, "Naomi and Ruth, this is a new beginning for you both." How aptly they depicted E.H. Swinstead's poem:

> There's a way back to God from the dark paths of sin;
> There's a door that is open and you may go in:
> At Calvary's cross is where you begin,
> When you come as a sinner to Jesus.

Paul combines the Lord Jesus Christ's fulfilment of these two memorable feasts in Philippians 3:10, and calls each of us to enter into their deep meaning by saying, *"that I may know Him and the power of His resurrection, and the fellowship of His sufferings."*

By the grace of God, many a drunkard was rescued through the ministry of the old Water Street Mission in New York. Sam Hadley was one who stumbled into it and was wonderfully saved as the result of hearing about the Saviour. He became so attached and involved in it that he ultimately became its Superintendent. When Charles Alexander visited the Mission, Sam Hadley took him to streets in Lower Manhattan to let him see the kind of circumstances in which men and women were living, to show him the effects of their depravity. After a lengthy walk, they reached the point where they parted and, being musically minded, Charles Alexander could hear the uneven gait of Sam Hadley walking in the other direction for he had an artificial limb. Suddenly it stopped, and when Alexander turned around he saw Sam Hadley leaning against a lamppost and hurried back, assuming that Hadley was sick. He reached him only to discover that he was pounding the lamppost with his fist and repeating, "O God, the sin of this city is breaking my heart. O God, the sin of this city is breaking my heart." In a very sensitive way he was entering into the fellowship of Christ's sufferings by showing how his heart was touched by the sin and needs of others, and longing for their deliverance just as he had known it from his past.

For Naomi and Ruth, their past was behind them too. As a returning Jew, it meant reconnecting with what she had forfeited during these empty years of her life. Coming back probably meant she was seeing it more meaningfully second time around and, like some brought up in a Christian home, she knew the reality of coming back to it for herself. For a Moabitess, as a Gentile, it meant being introduced to the truth of redemption and all that flows from it. It was a heart-searching reintroduction for Naomi, but for Ruth it must have felt like a heart-warming introduction to the service of God and she must have wondered what it was all about. Apart from sensing the people's appreciation of the Passover, the wave sheaf indicated that God had priority.

> O, wonder to myself I am
> That I can view the dying Lamb;
> Can scan the wondrous mystery o'er
> And not be moved to love Him more.
> (Joseph Denham Smith)

He was first, and the remainder was for the people's on-going satisfaction as they entered into their God-given blessing from the harvest. They had come into Bethlehem when its people were moved, not only in the sense that it was for them on their arrival, but by commemorating the Passover lamb and seeing the sheaf of the firstfruits offered to God. While this meant renewal for Naomi, it was entirely new for Ruth, yet for both of them Moab was over, Bethlehem was before them, and the Land of Israel in all its fulness was theirs to be enjoyed.

The Targum says, "They came to Bethlehem on the day in which the children of Israel began to mow the sheaf of barley which was to be waved before the Lord." This was called the *"sheaf of the firstfruits,"* and the festival was held on the day after the Sabbath following Passover,[27] on the first day of the week that pointed forward to His resurrection, and it was announcing that God was given first place. It must have been a heart-searching reintroduction for Naomi and a heart-warming welcome for Ruth who would learn the guiding principle - *"Honour the LORD with your possessions, and with the firstfruits of all your increase."*[28] Besides being the symbol of putting God first, the wave sheaf was the proof of more to come for the satisfaction of His people, not only of barley but also of the wheat.

These two crops were treated quite differently. Wheat was the preferred grain: its fineness enjoyed by the people and accepted by God for meal offerings on His altar.[29] Barley is a rougher grain and its Hebrew name, *s^e'orāh*, is related to the word *sa'ar*, which means rough or hairy. It was looked upon as a second-class grain, and considered poorer than wheat. This distinction is apparent in 1 Kings 4:22 and 28 where *"fine flour"* was brought to Solomon while *"barley"* was brought for the horses.

There are vivid scriptural examples of people being associated with its poverty, and Revelation 6:6 shows that it was considered being worth only one-third the value of wheat. In Numbers chapter 5:15, a unique meal offering of barley was associated with a woman whose morality was being questioned. Unlike the meal offering of fine flour in Leviticus 1, it had no oil and no frankincense on it, because it could never foreshadow the fruit of the Holy Spirit and the fragrance of Christ. These suitably belonged to the fineness of the wheat[30] as it represented *"the meekness and gentleness of Christ"*[31] in His righteous manhood, but were absent from the coarser barley that belonged to the offering of jealousy and the possible presence of sin.

Another example is found in the days of Elisha when he was brought twenty loaves of barley following a time of famine and, like the Lord's feeding of the multitude, they *"ate and had some left over."*[32] Then came the greatest feeding of all, when the Man who is the answer to the finest of the wheat took five barley loaves, gave thanks, distributed them: *"So when they were filled, He said to His disciples, 'Gather up the fragments that remain.'"*[33]

John is the only one who quotes Andrew's comment to the Lord: *"There is a lad here who has five barley loaves and two small fish,"* and we would well imagine Him thanking the lad and saying, 'I know what it's like for I was a Boy from a poor home too.' But He had come from much farther away, and with divine compassion He saw the gathering *"like sheep not having a shepherd."*[34] Who better to meet their need at Passover time than the Lamb who would take away the sin of the world on a later Passover and give Himself as the Good Shepherd. In answer to feeding the five thousand from Galilee and having twelve baskets remaining, and to feeding the four thousand from Tyre and Sidon and having seven large baskets left over, He went to the cross to demonstrate that He alone can meet the need of both Jew and Gentile.

In another portrayal of this, Naomi and Ruth came at a time that pointed to the poverty of Christ, and Ruth had no idea that she would feature in the ancestry of the Man of whom Scripture says, *"that though He was rich, yet for your sakes He became poor, that you through His poverty might become rich."*[35] He has been cut off in His death, raised in His glorious resurrection, and He has brought us into *"the beginning of the barley harvest."*

Her story, as we have already noted, was set against the background of *"the days when the judges ruled,"* one of whom was Gideon who lacked confidence when God wanted to use him against the Midianites. To reassure him, God sent him down to the enemy's camp where he overheard *"a man telling a dream to his companion"* about *"a loaf of barley bread"* that *"tumbled into the camp of Midian,"*[36] and the companion interpreted it as Gideon being the victor. At that moment, his fear fled, his faith was fanned, and worship replaced his worry. Seeing himself in the imagery of the barley loaf, he realised that God wanted to use the poverty of his inadequacy, and there's a lesson for all of us here. God would rather use the servant who feels inadequate than trust the battle to someone who feels up to the task.

Ruth's journey began with faith and ended in sight, she journeyed in hope and arrived at home. In these, she is such a graphic portrayal of the Christian's walk with the Lord. It also begins with faith and ends in sight; it begins with hope, and it ends at home! What a beginning! *"For by grace you have been saved through faith"*[37]; and we enjoy having fellowship with our Saviour, *"whom having not seen you love."*[38] However, He will come in fulfilment of our hope by which we await the *"glorious appearing of our great God and Saviour Jesus Christ."*[39] But our hope goes beyond that of seeing Him for John gives this wonderful assurance that *"when He is revealed, we shall be like Him, for we shall see Him as He is. And everyone who has this hope in Him purifies himself, just as He is pure."*[40] Ruth had hope, but ours is an incomparable hope: we will be *"at home with the Lord,"*[41] we will see Him, and we will be like Him. No wonder Paul says, *"Now hope does not disappoint."*[42] And if hope doesn't disappoint, neither will home! Our Bethlehemite is waiting to see the fulfilment of *"the hope of His calling."*[43] What a day that will be, when His hope and ours are simultaneously fulfilled at His coming!

BARLEY CAKES
The Midianite is in the land,
And Israel's hard bestead.
There's poverty on every hand,
And scarcity of bread:
But brawny Gideon bears at night
The threshing of his floor,
And by the winepress, out of sight,
Conceals his precious store.

How well his honest heart esteems
The food his God has given!
A plain unleavened cake he deems
Fit for a guest from Heaven.
Here is a man whom God can tell,
'Go thou in this thy might.'
Yes, Midian's tents shall prove how well
A 'barley cake' can fight!

A lesson learn from Gideon's floor:
Nutritious food for you
Is in the Word; abundance more
Than ever Canaan grew.
And if you wish to serve the Lord
(For still His foes assail),
If you would wish to use the Sword,
First learn to use the Flail!
(J.M.S. Tait)

7

BOAZ THE MAN OF GOD

"There was a relative of Naomi's husband, a man of great wealth, of the family of Elimelech. His name was Boaz. So Ruth the Moabitess said to Naomi, "Please let me go to the field, and glean heads of grain after him in whose sight I may find favour." And she said to her, "Go, my daughter." Then she left, and went and gleaned in the field after the reapers. And she happened to come to the part of the field belonging to Boaz, who was of the family of Elimelech. Now behold, Boaz came from Bethlehem, and said to the reapers, "The LORD be with you!" And they answered him, "The LORD bless you!" Then Boaz said to his servant who was in charge of the reapers, "Whose young woman is this?"

So the servant who was in charge of the reapers answered and said, "It is the young Moabite woman who came back with Naomi from the country of Moab. And she said, 'Please let me glean and gather after the reapers among the sheaves.' So she came and has continued from morning until now, though she rested a little in the house." Then Boaz said to Ruth, "You will listen, my daughter, will you not? Do not go to glean in another field, nor go from here, but stay close by my young women. Let your eyes be on the field which they reap, and go after them. Have I not commanded the young men not to touch you? And when you are thirsty, go to the vessels and drink from what the young men have drawn." So she fell on her face, bowed down to the ground, and said to him, *"Why have I found favour in your eyes, that you should take notice of me, since I am a foreigner?"* (Ruth 2:1-10).

* * *

It's not always easy to gauge someone's godliness, but there was something about the deportment of Boaz when he came into the field. Everyone was busy, yet they suddenly knew he was there, as he greeted them with, *"The LORD be with you!"* In a mutual sense of God's presence, they replied: *"The LORD bless you!"* It's a well-known adage that you don't get a second chance to create a first impression, and this was the first impression that Boaz made on the young foreigner from Moab. These were the first words she heard from him, and they let her know that the LORD had priority in his life. What a marvellous introduction to the spirituality of this man! Evidently, he set the tone and work ethic of his workforce, and Ruth would discover that it would be equally apparent in his conversations with her. As a man of God, he conducted himself and his work in a godly way, and did everything to safeguard his workers from discovering that if something is ethically wrong it can't be spiritually right. This work environment must have been way beyond anything Ruth ever anticipated when she said to Naomi on the old dirt road, *"your people shall be my people, and your God, my God."*

A horticultural grower was concerned at the abnormally slow growth of his plants and made all sorts of checks to find out the cause: insufficient feeding, a problem with hydroponics, pest control, etc. Everything was as it should be, and finally the cause was discovered. It was ventilation: the atmosphere was wrong. In his Bethlehem field, Boaz made sure that the atmosphere was right both for and among his workers, and he immediately ensured it was right for Ruth too. From the outset, he was a man for whom it was worth working and who set an example, even to present-day Christians, that we should *"work heartily, as for the Lord and not for men"*[1] and that the assembly's atmosphere must be right.

It was like this in the days of Nehemiah when they were building the wall. A variety of people gave an ideal example of unity in diversity: men and women, perfumers and goldsmiths, people and high priest, all with *"a mind to work."*[2] This is a fitting description of the mindset Boaz fostered among his reapers, and it filtered down to the gleaners, including Ruth. We could hardly read Nehemiah 3 and miss the constant repetition of the word *"next."* It seems rather ordinary, but it was an integral part of Nehemiah's strategy. Far from being like people waiting in line, where the call, 'Next," refers to whoever happens to follow, in wall-building it meant something much more meaningful. These were not independent contributors. For them, "Next" was a call to blend with those on either side. Stonework must be carefully placed, and interlocking, and the work would show the inter-relationship of the workers.

The little word *'al* can simply mean "after," but in Leviticus 5:13 some versions speak of atonement being made *"for"* the person's sin. Other versions say *"touching"* or *"concerning,"* and we can readily understand the proximity intended by *'al.* However, the implications were very real for Nehemiah's builders. Each set must combine with those on their left and right to show that they are not only "next," but "for" and "touching" and "concerned" with their work. Side by side, shoulder-to-shoulder, it meant integration, until, firstly, *"the wall was joined together up to half its height."* As the workers, so the work: it was "joined together" in a real demonstration of equality. Everyone pulled their weight. There wasn't a bit of wall at one height and another bit at a different height. Men and women worked together in such a fashion that the whole thing was level. Isn't that how it should be for us too?

Complainers don't make good builders for their tendency is for the tongue to be in sympathy with an active mind and inactive hands to be in sympathy with their over-active tongues. Building is the ideal means of showing the equality or inequality of work rate, and it may be worth trying to deduce soberly before the Lord if an assembly would be better or worse off if everyone worked at your personal level. Building for God should mean togetherness; and pulling our weight is better than dragging our feet, and yet it's possible to be in a church where a core pulls its weight and a fringe drags its feet. Before the Lord, which group are we in? If you are on the fringe, please take this as a word from the Lord. He wants to draw you into the core to be a builder and worker among His people.

Nehemiah had a deep appreciation of doing what God wanted him to do, and so did Boaz. Naomi had heard that God had visited His people by giving them bread and a field of barley ready to be reaped was the evidence that He had. He had blessed, and also had arranged for Boaz to be a blessing. Leviticus 19:9 and 10 was a word from God to him: *"When you reap the harvest of your land, you shall not wholly reap the corners of your field, nor shall you gather the gleanings of your harvest ... you shall leave them for the poor and the stranger."* This made Ruth doubly qualified, but what about Naomi? A caring God provided for her by adding, *"When you reap your harvest in your field, and forget a sheaf in the field, you shall not go back to get it; it shall be for the stranger, the fatherless, and the widow, that the LORD your God may bless you in all the work of your hands."*[3] So Naomi could have been in that field as well, for there was provision for the widow as well as the stranger to be blessed through Boaz.

Whether she had tutored Ruth regarding the stranger's entitlement and the forgotten sheaf, we don't know, but Boaz certainly turned the law of the unintentional into intentional grace by ordering extra bundles for her. It's not something that fits with life on the farm nowadays for it wouldn't be good farming practice to forget a bale, or a sheaf in earlier days, for some sharp-eyed observer who could benefit. However, under the law, the widow could be blessed through man's forgetfulness, while an intentionally mindful God was watching the widow by watching the forgotten sheaf. Nevertheless, even though the sheaf had been left behind through forgetfulness, Boaz and others like him left it where it stood through their mindfulness for the law of God. By so doing, it became a provision of grace. How beautiful! He had promised Abraham that He would bless others by blessing him,[4] but His promise to Boaz was that he would be blessed by blessing others. It's worth noting that while blessing could come through being forgetful under law, we are under grace and blessing comes by remembering.

Acts 20:35: *"I have shown you in every way, by labouring like this, that you must support the weak. And remember the words of the Lord Jesus, that He said, 'It is more blessed to give than to receive.'"*

Galatians 2:10: *"They desired only that we should remember the poor, the very thing which I also was eager to do."*

2 Peter 1:13: *"Yes, I think it is right, as long as I am in this tent, to stir you up by reminding you ..."*

Hebrews 13:2: *"Do not forget to entertain strangers ..."*

Hebrews 13:16: *"But do not forget to do good and to share, for with such sacrifices God is well pleased."*

As Boaz greeted his workers, he noticed a figure he didn't recognise and immediately turned to his servant who was *"in charge"* of the reapers. This is interesting. The man wasn't described as a manager or by rank. He was approached on the basis of his relationship to Boaz and to the workers. He was *"hannitstsab 'al"* or "set over," which tells us that Boaz had appointed a man who was in touch with him and his workers. He proved this by what he knew about Ruth: he knew where she came from and who brought her; he knew why she had come, and he had noted her commitment, so he was a servant and observant!

There's no doubt that he had been promoted, but he didn't lose his servant status in the process, and neither do we. It's a poor response to divine recognition if a brother appointed as an elder sees it as a promotion in rank rather than of personal relationship. All servants will not be elders, but all elders should be servants. Boaz's right-hand man was his "next" in line, and so he asked him, *"Whose young woman is this?"* He didn't ask, "Who is this young woman?" These are two very different questions. In fact, they are two different kinds of question. His way of asking showed that he was interested in possession not pedigree. Position and status can be valued as well-earned in life, and well-handled too, but are worth very little if we are not among those of whom Paul said, *"The Lord knows those who are His."*[5]

Boaz was like Eliezer when Abraham sent him to bring a bride home for Isaac. When he met Rebekah at the well and asked, *"Whose daughter are you?"*[6] he wanted to know her possession. Likewise, when David came to Elah and conquered Goliath, Saul was so keen to find out *"Whose son is this youth?"*[7] he asked the question three times. David's answer was very humble for a young man who had just rid the king and his army of a terrorising giant: *"I am the son of your servant Jesse the Bethlehemite."* There it is again: "your servant," and, presenting himself as the nameless son of the Bethlehemite, making himself of no reputation. No wonder God called him *"a man after My own heart."*[8] Jesus was the true 'house of bread-ite' and His servants should take character from Him.

Ruth belonged to Moab. She was a Moabite by birth and a Moabite by nature, but she became a Bethlehemite by grace and favour and knew that it's better to be poor in Bethlehem than rich in Moab. When the servant witnessed to how busily she had gleaned, he mentioned that she had *"rested a little in the house."* As lord of the harvest, Boaz had provided a shack - it may even have been a tent for workers to go to eat and to shelter. It was a place of rest and refreshment and at some point perhaps in the heat of noon Ruth went there to rest, which was far better than trying to find rest in the house of her husband. Wycliffe points out that the Septuagint translation says, "She has not rested (even) a little in the field."

When Naomi told both girls that the Lord would deal kindly with them and give them rest, it was a rather hollow and meaningless assurance, but it was meaningful in this little place in the house of bread. Boaz wanted to set her mind at rest too, and his request must have sounded more like a statement than a question: *"You will listen, my daughter, will you not?"* Then he added, *"Do not go to glean in another field, nor go from here, but stay close to my young women. Let your eyes be on the field which they reap, and go after them."*

In fixing her direction, he fixed her position, but it was for her to fix her attention on what was his and have communion with those who were his: *"my young women ... my young men ... my harvest."* As the story progressed, he also spoke of *"my town"* and *"my people,"* but the sweetest of all was at the beginning when he called her *"my daughter"* and at the end when he owned her as *"my wife."* By asking her to focus on what was his, and on those who were his, he wanted her to feel included and to know that he had expectations of her. The Lord Jesus has done much more for us. He is interested in our position and says, *"Abide in Me, and I in you. As the branch cannot bear fruit of itself, unless it abides in the vine, neither can you, unless you abide in Me."*[9] He has fixed our position, and is worthy of our lifelong direction, affection, attention and communion.

Boaz cautioned her against being distracted and going elsewhere to *"another field."* For us as disciples of the Lord Jesus Christ, there also is the lure of another field. He said, *"The field is the world,"*[10] and although we are in it we are not of it.[11] He has set our direction. For this reason, He has given us rest to keep us at rest by graciously urging us, *"Do not love the world or the things in the world."*[12] He has set our affection. He also leaves us in no doubt that *"the lust of the flesh, the lust of the eye, and the pride of life – is not of the Father."*[13] He has set our attention. We are told in Proverbs that *"The righteous should choose his friends carefully,"*[14] and Psalm 119 directs us to say, *"I am a companion of all who fear You."* He has set our communion.

Ruth had been called into the godly atmosphere of Boaz's field, and he commanded the young men not to touch her. As a man of God, he was rich in morality and his young men were expected to be the same. They were under orders not to touch her, so she was safeguarded from being plagued by them. The New Testament lifts up the same kind of example for believers in Paul's advice to Timothy to treat older women as mothers and the younger woman as sisters. This is part of the New Testament's protection for young men towards young women, that no worldly code of conduct will be brought into the service of God, and nothing contrary to the mind of God to challenge the morality of the

Word of God. The moral climate of our world is geared to distract young Christians and tempt them to accept its norms as theirs, but the Lord Jesus is looking for purity and has the ability to conquer the power of fleshly desires in us.

Ruth was encouraged by the man who would become her redeemer, but, young Christian, you are being encouraged by the Man who is your Redeemer. He has already paid for you, so that allows Him to say, *"You were bought at a price, therefore glorify God in your body."* If an Old Testament redeemer could say it to Ruth, then your Redeemer has far more right to say it to you, so that the purity of young people will be kept intact for Jesus' sake.

The reason He redeemed you is that God will confirm His purpose by saying, *"But know that the LORD has set apart for Himself him who is godly."*[15] Perhaps, as you read this, He actually wants to say to you, "You will listen, will you not?" He is making an appeal for you to commit yourself to Him and be separated to Him. It's often called being sanctified, and this means being set apart as holy. This is how the English Standard Version translates Paul's appeal in 2 Timothy 2:21 – *"Therefore, if anyone cleanses himself from what is dishonourable he will be a vessel for honourable use, set apart as holy, useful to the master of the house, ready for every good work."* To be practical about it, cleansing ourselves means saying "No" to sin. To Peter, this meant abstaining;[16] to Paul, it meant killing off the impulse and the action;[17] to us, it means both.

God wants our fleshly desires, and tendencies, and habits to be put to death for, if we don't kill them, they will kill off your walk with the Lord and your work for Him. Boaz had Ruth's interests and wellbeing at heart when he asked her to listen, and what he said didn't come across to her as an ultimatum. He called her *"my daughter"* and that was special. Years later, David included the word for daughter when he prayed, *"Keep me as the apple of Your eye,"* which can be translated as "Guard me as the pupil, daughter of the eye." God has designed our eyes in such a way that the pupils are protected by surrounding bone structure, our eyebrows, eyelids, eyelashes, and by tears. It's in such tenderness that God protects us and makes His appeal.

If ever anyone met an appeal with a proper response, it was Ruth for *"she fell on her face and bowed down to the ground."* At that moment, she took her place among the greats of the Bible. Abraham heard the voice of God and fell on his face in obedience.[18] Ezekiel received the vision from the throne of God and fell on his face in wonder and worship.[19] Daniel saw and heard the vision of future events and fell on his face in reverence and in godly fear.[20] In her first day of gleaning, and first response to the man who would mean more and more to her as the days went by, Ruth set an example of humility for us all. Following it, we bow before a worthier Redeemer.

From her lowly position, Boaz filled her horizon. Does the Lord Jesus Christ do that for me? Does He fill your horizon? The beginning of Romans 1 says He should. He is *"of the seed of David according to the flesh, and declared to be the Son of God with power."* John 1:18 tells us that *"No one has seen God at any time. The only begotten Son, who is in the bosom of the Father, He has declared Him."* Uniquely, Jesus is the exposition, the full explanation or the exegesis of God. When Paul referred to the One who is *"declared to be the Son of God with power,"* it's very fitting that the Spirit of God gave him a different word, and from it we get our word "horizon." The Son fills His Father's horizon, and we are blessed in having the opportunity to let Him fill our vision too. Rainbows often appear as vertical full circles to hill climbers and as horizontal circles that aeroplane passengers can see in the clouds below. The spectacle is known as 'a glory' and, remarkably, the climber's image and the image of the aeroplane appears in the middle of the circle.

As we close this chapter, please let me ask you if your Redeemer is your glory? Maybe you are wondering how you can reach that point. Take the lowly place and let Him fill your horizon and, like John the Baptist, say, *"He must increase, but I must decrease."*[21] Our highest place is lying low at our Redeemer's feet.

> Be thou my vision, O Lord of my heart;
> Naught be all else to me, save that thou art -
> Thou my best thought, by day or by night;
> Waking or sleeping, thy presence my light.
>
> Be thou my wisdom, and thou my true word;
> I ever with thee and thou with me, Lord.
> Thou my great Father; thine own may I be,
> Thou in me dwelling and I one with thee.
>
> Riches I heed not, nor vain, empty praise;
> Thou mine inheritance, now and always;
> Thou and thou only first in my heart,
> High King of heaven, my treasure thou art.
>
> High King of heaven, my victory won,
> May I reach heaven's joys, O bright heaven's sun!
> Heart of my own heart, whatever befall,
> Still be my vision, O Ruler of all.
> *(Dallan Forgaill (530-598)*
> *(Adapted Eleanor Henrietta Hull (1860-1935))*

8

IN HIS FIELD

"So she gleaned in the field until evening, and beat out what she had gleaned, and it was about an ephah of barley" (Ruth 2:17).

* * *

The most momentous hours this world has ever known were nine o'clock in the morning and three o'clock in the afternoon. Outside Jerusalem on Calvary's Hill at nine o clock in the morning, soldiers hammered nails through the Lord Jesus' hands and feet, raised the cross and jolted it into a socket in the ground. It wasn't by chance: His timing was perfect, and when it came to three o'clock in the afternoon the Saviour said, "It is finished!" His sufferings were over.

The world didn't know it then, but these hours combined the cruelty of men and the kindness of God: their hatred and His love, their wilfulness and His will. In such a brutal way, men fulfilled what He had been writing about for centuries, and then confirmed through Peter on the Day of Pentecost: *"Him, being delivered by the determined purpose and foreknowledge of God, you have taken by lawless hands, have crucified, and put to death."*[1] There are no accidents with God, and men unknowingly complied with His timetable of morning and evening!

God loves painting pictures. In Genesis, His creation was woven around the daily timing of *"evening ['ereb] and morning [boqer]."*[2] Annually, in commemoration of Exodus 12, the Passover lamb was killed at evening as the introduction to the Feasts of Jehovah and as a constant reminder to the people of Israel's redemption from bondage in Egypt. In Exodus 29, the timing of each day's service in the tabernacle was built around *"One lamb you shall offer in the morning [from boqer], and the other lamb you shall offer in the evening [from 'ereb]."*

This was God's way of ensuring that His people's daily walk was regulated by the prominence of the lamb. The conduct of each day began with the offering of the morning lamb, and God was left with the evening lamb burning before Him in the silence of each night. In the context of these lambs, God made it known: *"I will meet with the children of Israel, and the tabernacle shall be sanctified by My glory."*[3]

Thus God completes the triplet of creation, redemption and sanctification by referring to morning and evening. In His divine artistry, was He not painting vivid portrayals of what He would achieve through the cross of His Son? Was He not anticipating the cross-centeredness of our new creation in Christ,[4] our redemption,[5] and our sanctification,[6] so that all we have from Him, and are for Him, is through the Lamb?

Ruth's Evening and Morning

When Ruth went looking for work, she was looking for more than a barley field. God had planted a thought in her heart that guided her feet for she wanted to find someone who would show grace. God honoured her desire, yet the record simply says, *"And she happened to come to the part of the field belonging to Boaz."* We could be inclined to interpret this as 'accidentally by accident,' but closer thought will help us to see it was by appointment and not by accident. It was as if she lived out Solomon's thoughts generations before he was alive: *"Keep your heart with all diligence ... Let your eyes look straight ahead ... Ponder the path of your feet."*[7]

There's no doubt that Ruth's heart, eyes and feet were in unison, but this doesn't explain how *"she happened to come"* to the field that was owned by a close relative, though this latter part had probably never entered her mind. No, for all unknown to her was the loftier thought that she had found grace in the eyes of God, and He was seeing her at the centre of her future grandson's promise, *"The steps of a good (wo)man are ordered by the LORD."*[8] This helps us to understand *wayyiqer miqrehā*— she happened to come. Some older versions say, *"her hap was to light on"* (ASV, RV), while the NIV translates the phrase as, *"As it turned out."* But who made it turn out so favourably? Ruth was yet to discover that the One who called her from Moab, who gave her the right words to say when Orpah turned back, was the One now leading her forward into far greater things.

The truth is that just as Naomi was able to acknowledge that *"the LORD brought me home,"* so Ruth ultimately would realise that God had brought this about for her. He was working out His purpose, and it's interesting that both words in *wayyiqer miqrehā* are linked to the thought of framing timbers. As we know, roof trusses don't just happen, they are planned; and bringing them together is by choice, not chance. In bringing Ruth to this field, God was intentionally laying the beams that would structure her future. Her life was under construction, and soon she would sense that her choice was within His choice.

How blessed we are when our hearts, eyes and feet conjoin and cause us to know that things happen when we allow God to order our steps and frame His plan for us. It's by His leading we also recognise His grace in bringing our thoughts and ways into alignment with His own, and find that our lives are being constructed according to His plan. It was by gleaning that Ruth found out more about this mighty man of wealth, and it's by patient and prayerful gleaning that we also deepen our bond with the Lord Jesus Christ. There's something so valuable in having someone ask, as Naomi asked Ruth, *"Where have you gleaned today?"*[9] It was gleaning that kept her going, and kept her sharing what she gathered, and it's like that for us too. Fellow-Christian, beware the danger of not gleaning daily from your Bible!

Bit-by-bit, God led her to experience a deepening and more reliant bond with Boaz that illustrates the kind of relationship we are able to have with our Saviour. His call to us is, *"Take My yoke upon you and learn from Me,"*[10] but there's no learning without gleaning. For Ruth, that meant being in the field day after day. That's where she found him; and for us it means being in the Word every day for that's where we glean and enjoy communion with Christ. The same unchanging God who was in control in her life wants to be in control of our lives today, tomorrow, and every day, but we need to turn up for work!

Until evening

Evening brings us back to the word *'ereb*, the time when the lamb was placed on the altar, and to a time that would be fixed in a godly Jew's mind. What a way to conclude the day, with thoughts of the lamb! But Ruth's day wasn't finished. With her gleaning over, it was time to *"beat out what she had gleaned,"*[11] and the gleaner became the beater. This was when the stalks revealed their fruitfulness, and the quantity of grain she took home after separating it from the chaff.

Her diligent effort reminds us of what it took for gleaning and beating to be turned into feeding and sets a good example for our daily reading that we meditate on it until we derive nourishment and satisfaction from it. We could put it this way: there should always be something of the "evening" in the character of what we draw from studying the Scriptures. All our consideration should lead us to the Lamb, for our thoughts will never mature until they converge with His.

Ruth's whole aim was to carry home the finished product of her gleaning, and not devote unnecessary effort on carrying straw. This is particularly relevant to those who share in the ministry of preaching and teaching. Long hours go into gathering our thoughts while preparing a message, yet its presentation will be much shorter. We do well to catch the essence of Old Testament men like Malachi who passed on what they called *"The burden of the word of the LORD."* Naomi was fed by Ruth's burden, not with bulky straw. How noticeable it is that chapters 2 and 3 end with Naomi's response to what she had brought, and both times she spoke about *"This man"* or *"the man."* It was the best of all conclusions. During the day, Ruth's eyes were fixed on the field; at night, they were fixed on the man. What a goal for preachers of God's Word! Our messages should be chaff-free.

The one who permitted and enabled Ruth's burden became the focus of their conversation, not the good barley. How much more Christ-exalting when a message prompts God's people to speak of their Redeemer rather than merely to say, "Good message." It's of necessity that the speaker prepares by gathering thoughts from the Word, but its presentation should cause our brothers and sisters to gather thoughts of the Lord. Sadly, we need much of the Spirit's help to separate the chaff for books and songbooks in Christian bookshops are not always chaff-free. God's people deserve to hear *"the word of the message,"*[12] but they won't know until the message has been delivered whether the speaker had his hands full of roasted grain or bales of straw!

At home on the farm, there's a well-known saying when building a dry-stone wall: "Don't lift the same stone twice." The aim is lift it and place it, and the stone will tell you by sound and feel that it's where it should be. This was never in Ruth's mind. She must have handled the same grain at least four or five times: gleaning, beating, carrying, milling and cooking. She well and truly made it her own. Should we ever think that the counsel of His will is finished with us when we glean? Far from it! There's much more to it that that. We may be blessed in gleaning, even publicly at the feet and in fellowship with others, but beating is a more private matter. Meditation is a deeply personal exercise, and it's vital that each of us learns to think proper thoughts of God, His Son, and of His Word.

Just as every infant masters the art of feeding, and leaving behind the early stages of being spoon-fed, the child of God must develop his or her early pickings by beating, carrying, milling and preparing what he or she has gleaned. When we come to Christ, we are like Ruth. We pick things up about Him like a stalk here and there; gradually learning about Him, being attracted to Him, wanting to be fed and satisfied by Him. We gather something and enjoy handling it for the first time, then we handle it again as we think it over, and this leads on to meditative thoughts for worship that we give to God.

In the process of making it our own, it may become something we want to pass on to others privately by letter or in conversation; or publicly in Sunday School, Bible Class or in a church gathering. By whatever opportunity the Lord gives, we can share Paul's mutual desire, *"that I may come to you with joy by the will of God, and may be refreshed together with you,"*[13] and someone might encourage you by assuring you that *"the hearts of the saints have been refreshed by you."*[14] They may not have watched you gleaning and gathering, but they will hear the evidence that you did.

Boaz watched Ruth as she gleaned. We can imagine why he kept his eye on the reapers, but he showed an added concern for her. Having thanked him for his grace he expressed it still further by inviting her, *"Come here, and eat of the bread, and dip your piece of bread in the vinegar."* Allowing her to sit with reapers was one way of showing acceptance, but to be within hand's reach of him was like a foreshadowing of Christians knowing they are *"accepted in the Beloved."*[15] She was among workers who began their day by saying to Boaz, "The LORD bless you!" but now he was blessing her. He had already provided water to quench her thirst, but now she had the added benefit of the vinegar, which was refreshing in the heat of the day. He had told her to "dip" her bread into it, which was his way of saying, "Immerse it. Plunge it in. Don't just slightly moisten it. Get the full benefit, and be refreshed."

Then his hand reached out to her with a handful of parched grain. It had been gathered and beaten out, separated from the chaff and roasted. He had handled it and wanted to share it personally with her. It's the only time in the Old Testament where the word *tsābat* is used and it was reserved for the lord of the harvest reaching out to a stranger. This was grain that had passed through the fire, and she took it from his hand. She gleaned with her own hands, and gathered what other hands let fall for her,[16] but no one else in the field ever put something into her hand. He gave it to her and it was like eating out of his hand. Ruth enjoyed what she gleaned for herself. She was blessed when others left handfuls for her, but getting something from his hand was best of all.

Is there a sequel to this for us? Oh, yes! We enjoy what we glean from the Word, and often are blessed by what others share from their study of it, but there's nothing like receiving a word from the Lord. In all your reading and study of God's Word, gather all you can and let others give all they can, but never stop there. Ask for new thoughts that are from Him for nothing compares with the experience of Jesus putting something into your hand.

Be comfortable in His presence and wait until you are eating out of His hand. He is the answer to the roasted grain, because it speaks of the intensity of the cross and all He endured in those three hours of darkness from midday to three o'clock in the afternoon, when at evening He said, "It is finished!" This is where we began our Christian walk, isn't it?

> I stood one day at Calvary
> Where Jesus bled and died,
> I never knew He loved me so,
> For me was crucified;
> And as I stood there in my sin,
> His love reached down to me,
> And O the shame that filled my soul
> That day at Calvary!
> (Walter H. Huntley)

Boaz put so much into her hand that she couldn't finish it for *"she ate and was satisfied, and kept some back."*[17] She had gathered an ephah of barley, between twenty and twenty-five pounds in weight, and Naomi must have wondered at such productive gleaning. But no gleaner ever gleaned roasted barley. It was the proof of sitting with him. She showed no reluctance in reaching out to his giving hand. When Christ reaches out to you are you prepared to reach out to Him? He always gives more than we need, and never gives short measure.

My brother and sister, in whatever way the Lord calls you to share something from His Word, others will know when you have been sitting with Him. When it happens, the proof will always be there. Again, it's how we started. When God saved us, He *"made us alive together with Christ ... and raised us up together, and made us to sit together in the heavenly places in Christ Jesus."*[18] We are already with Him. We are within hand's reach of Him, so we should let others see, not only what we are in Christ, but where we are in Christ. Naomi could tell that Ruth had been with Boaz, and others should see that we have been with Jesus.

The word *qāliy* is translated as "parched grain" six times in the Old Testament, but the closely associated *qālāh* is translated as "base, despised, and seem vile," while David applied it to himself when he spoke of being *"lightly esteemed."*[19] The first reference to parched grain is found in Leviticus 23:14 in connection with the wave sheaf of the feast of firstfruits: *"You shall eat neither bread nor parched grain nor fresh grain until the same day that you have brought an offering to your God."* We also read in Joshua 5:11 that, when he led the people over Jordan into Gilgal, they ate *"unleavened bread and parched grain"*[20] on the day after the Passover; so the parched grain, the lamb and the wave sheaf were closely linked.

This leads us to conclude that Boaz had honoured God by keeping the Passover and offering his wave sheaf before giving Ruth a handful of parched grain. This was a very meaningful way of showing to the young Gentile that she had been brought into the grace that comes by honouring the law. There seems to be a precious lesson here for us, too. The roasted grain wasn't eaten in association with the lamb, which portrayed the death of Christ, but following the wave sheaf that spoke of His resurrection. It wasn't linked to the grief of the One who was despised, humiliated on a cross as if he were evil, and lightly esteemed, but with the triumph of His ascension in glory. This is so significant for it means we feed on the sufficiency of His sufferings in the light of owning the power of His resurrection. As He gives us thoughts, consideration of His anguish doesn't leave us in mourning, but rather lifts us upward to worship God for the Victor. In our equivalent of the roasted grain, we lovingly dwell on His grief, but He puts His glory into our hands. Just as Boaz did with Ruth, Jesus wants to put them into your hand and into your home. As dear William Blane said so ably of Him:

> Man of slighted Nazareth,
> King who wore the thorny wreath,
> Son obedient unto death,
> He shall bear the glory.

* * *

> It is coming, it is coming, sure and bright,
> Through His grace;
> That day when faith shall turn to sight
> In yon place.
> Where we'll tread the golden street
> And at last fit praise repeat,
> While we cast crowns at His feet
> Face to face.

The face where Mary's sorrow drew forth tears,
We shall see;
At the feet that journeyed for us all those years
We shall be.
Feet that never rested yet,
Face that ever steadfast set,
'Till He paid our dreadful debt
On the tree.

Now 'tis finished, He's in glory, and we wait,
Where He's been.
Till His own hand leads us through the heavenly gate
Of yon scene.
Every step through desert sands,
He had trod and understands,
'Tis on strong and tender hands
That we lean.

Oh, the grace that made His holy head once bow,
Death to meet;
Ne'er forgets us in the glory where He now
Has His seat;
'Tis the love that made Him die,
Sought us, found us, keeps us nigh,
Will be rapture by and by
At His feet.
(Miss Ora Rowan)

9

AT HIS FEET

"So she lay at his feet until morning, and she arose before one could recognize another. Then he said, "Do not let it be known that the woman came to the threshing floor." Also he said, "Bring the shawl that is on you and hold it." And when she held it, he measured six ephahs of barley, and laid it on her. Then she went into the city" (Ruth 3:14,15).

* * *

So far, the chapters open and close with remarkable contrasts, and this chapter continues this process. Chapter 1 begins with Elimelech and others leaving Bethlehem in a time of famine and ends with his widow and Ruth returning there in a time of plenty. Chapter 2 introduces us to Boaz who stayed in Bethlehem in spite of the famine and concludes with Ruth working for him in his harvest fields. Now, chapter 3 begins with the promise of Ruth the poor stranger finding rest, and closes with him not finding rest until she is assured of a rich redeemer. In the purpose of God, she is moving on from being the gleaner who enjoyed looking for provision to become the partner who enjoyed loving the provider. So this *"rest"* is linked to finding a husband in accordance with God's law, and Naomi's dependence on Boaz fulfilling the right of redemption and marriage.[1]

My daughter, shall I not seek security for you ...?

This *"security"* is very different from the *"rest"* Naomi had in mind in chapter 1:9 when she urged Ruth and Orpah to *"find rest, each in the house of her husband."* Moab was incapable of giving *"rest"* that would allow it to *"be well"* with her. Naomi had learned the hard way that true happiness belonged to being among God's people, and He was about to make things *"well"* for Ruth by bringing her to the feet of the man who was *"cheerful,"*[2] which encourages us to think she was about to enter into the joy of her lord. Both words are based on the same Hebrew word, *yātab*, and Ruth was about to discover that her wellbeing, joy and contentment were all bound up in him. Successive chapters show their developing bond. In chapter 2, she entered into his work in the field. In chapter 3, she entered into his rest at his feet. And chapter 4 will see her entering into his home. What a wonderful progression! In the field, she saw loose stalks and bound sheaves, but at his feet she saw the garnered harvest in its entirety. As Christians, we have the joy of being given *"rest"* and of continuing to find it as we serve Him. Ruth also had a developing rest, and we see this in verse 18 when Naomi urged her to *"sit still"* for she considered Boaz as being the resting place for her.

Boaz was the key to both doors, to redemption and rest, and Naomi could see the possibility of a complete new future for Ruth in him. She was so fully acquainted with his whereabouts that she could advise Ruth to be involved in what he was doing *"tonight."* No reaper is named, Ruth is the only named gleaner, and Boaz himself is the winnower. Winnowing separates the barley and wheat from the chaff and, in Israel, an evening breeze comes in from the sea and he would see the benefit of this as he tossed the grain into the wind for it to remove the light chaff. For maximum benefit, the threshing floor would be located on an exposed place outside the village on the side of a hill or at its top. To reach it Ruth had to "*go down*" the hills on which Bethlehem stands.

This is confirmed in chapter 4:1 where it says, "*Boaz went up to the gate*" after parting from Ruth at the threshing floor. Threshing floors are among God's landmarks that pointed to Calvary, as we will see in chapter 14. Grain is one of God's beaten things, and different instruments fulfil a range of work: the flail for grain, the mortar for manna, the hammer for gold, the press for olives, and the feet for grapes. How meaningfully He implemented each one to produce feeding, adorning, enlightening and rejoicing, and all are fulfilled in Christ for the enriching of our lives.

Therefore wash yourself ... anoint ... put on your best garment and go

Coming into his presence called for preparation, and approaching his feet called for more personal examination than being in the field. There was a proper way to approach the lord of the harvest: not with the stench of the day's sweat or in old working clothes. By removing the filthiness of the flesh, bearing a fragrance, and looking her best, Ruth had no other motive but to do her utmost for him. We see her readiness, her reverence and her rest, as a bride prepared for marriage.

She washed

Her purity was of first importance for she wanted to be appealing. Naturally speaking, it was pointless to wash before going to the dusty, cloudy atmosphere of the threshing floor, but Ruth washed herself[3] for the person not the place. By doing this, she gave the right spiritual lesson for those who want to live in the unclouded atmosphere of the Christ of the cross. Having fellowship with Him, first of all, means being fully bathed – *leloumenos* from *louō*, washed all over[4] because of the Word.[5]

She anointed

This was her sanctity, since she wanted to be appropriate, but her purity was the essential foundation of her sanctity. There can't be sanctification without purification, and it's vital we know that being sanctified flows from being purified. Defilement can never be anointed![6] Nor can it be covered up. Fragrance can't adorn filth, just as faith can't condone the flesh. Naturally, perfume can be applied to an unwashed skin, but it's scent will be compromised by the admixture. Sanctity depends on purity, and God's holiness demands that His will cannot use what His Word hasn't washed!

She put on

This was her dignity for she wanted his approval. It meant setting aside the widow's foreign garb of Moab and the working clothes of the field and wearing what many versions call her "best clothes."[7] Garments in Scripture often refer to testimony. Ruth had a good one, and she wanted to be at her best for him. As we thought in the seventh chapter of our study in Jude, this particular word for *"garment"* (*kasalmāh* from *salmāh* and *simlāh*) means 'a dress that takes shape from what is under it.' The word is used in Psalm 104:2 where the psalmist spoke to God as the One *"who cover Yourself with light as with a garment."* As we thought then, he was speaking of God's pre-bodily form and thinking of a garment taking shape, not from His body, but from His Being. Apart altogether from what she was wearing under her shawl, from a spiritual point of view,

Ruth was at Boaz's feet in her "best garment," for even the darkness of night couldn't hide the light of her inner character that shaped and commended her testimony to him. He was touched by what he saw in her, and she was touched by what she saw in him.

We speak about having contacts, and of people having contact with us, but what does it really mean to be 'in touch,' and with what are they 'in touch'? Hopefully, it's not only with the 'outer me,' otherwise the benefit will be poor and short-lived. It's in touching others and in them being in touch with our *"inner man"* (Eph.3:16) that they will be in touch and be touched by Christ-likeness. If friends come to us for advice, let it be the Wonderful Counsellor they reach for and not our limited counselling. When they come in their times of sorrow, let it be the Comforter who reaches out to them and not merely the hand of our limited consolation. It's equally important when correction or judgment is needed, and this includes assembly matters, fragile situations call for Christlike care and not for uncaring Christians. Loved ones should always know that they are being helped by those whose garment of testimony resembles the Lord's in that it takes shape from what there is of Him in us.

She went down

This was her humility for she wanted his acceptance. The gleaner of the field was still in lowly deference at his feet. Just as sanctity is repelled by impurity, humility is repelled by pride. Haughtiness is no companion of holiness, and those who are high-minded never fill the lowly place. There was nothing haughty about Ruth. All Boaz's acts of kindness in the field hadn't made her the slightest bit pompous or obnoxious. As he had humbled himself to care for her, so she humbled herself to be with him. God never ceases to be the High and Lofty One,[8] and we should never cease to be *"clothed with humility."*[9]

She came softly

This was her propriety. There was no flamboyant entrance; no noisy or clumsy access. She came secretly and silently,[10] and never drew attention to herself or advertised what she was doing. She knew how to approach him, and the lessons pour out of her to help us see how to do the right thing in the right way. All four parts of her preparation contributed to this. There was softness in her spirit long before there was softness in her steps. It was good that she came, but how she came was better. We should know and show that spiritual service is not all about "me." Drawing near to God calls for spiritual caution.

Perhaps it's worth asking ourselves, "If we were to come like Old Testament offerers, would we be allowed in?" Reverence is vital, and so is standing in awe. The psalmist had it right when he said, *"Let all the inhabitants of the world stand in awe of Him."*[11] We draw near to pour out our hearts in prayer, but it's not a wake; and we draw near to worship and celebrate, yet it's not unruly. We should never allow a sense of familiarity to creep into our approach to God. Better to say, and mean it, *"I will go softly all my years."*[12] Jacob showed similar caution in Genesis 33:14 when he promised Esau that he would *"lead on slowly"* out of consideration for the children and livestock. Christ-like gentleness calls for reverence and deference in His followers, leaders, and preachers. Followers must learn the proper approach, and so must leaders and preachers. Humility is the hallmark of each and will save them from all sorts of hurt and harm, not least where pride can mar not only the approach, but also the outcome. Such was the case for a preacher whose apparently proud approach caused an elderly sister to observe, "If you had gone up the way you came down, you would have come down the way you went up!"

Did God gently rebuke Naomi when Ruth said, *"All that you say to me I will do"?* It was like an echo of His people's promise at Sinai[13] and should have been a reminder of her national obligation to covenant law and love. Ruth's pledge was acceptable conduct for the threshing floor, and a fitting pointer to the One who would say, *"I have finished the work which You have given Me to do."*[14]

where he lies ... lie down

Repeating the same Hebrew verb implied making the place of his rest her rest, of finding his rest and entering into it by doing what he had done. What an exemplary flow there is in verses 3-7: *"go down ... lie down ... went down ... lay down"!* She claimed the place of his wife by sharing his blanket, but being at his feet signified that she didn't yet have this status. There was no immoral standard implied in her action, and no damage done to their reputations. Their behaviour was consistent with a godly line. As lord of the harvest, Boaz was rejoicing in his harvest. His work was over and he had cause to rest in it with joy. In this we see something of the One who said, *"It is finished!"* and who endured everything *"for the joy that was set before Him."*[15]

Once again, it was as if she were entering into the joy of her lord,[16] but he was startled when he suddenly awoke and found her there. His question was different from what he asked on her first day in the field. Then, it was, *"Whose young woman is this?"* But now it was simply, *"Who are you?"* He was more interested in "Who?" than "Whose?" because she had spread part of his blanket over her to indicate her wish for marriage. Her response confirmed this: *"Spread your wings over your servant, for you are a redeemer."*[17] Adam Clarke says in his commentary:

95

"The wing is the emblem of protection ... The meaning is, Take me to thee for wife; and so the Targum translated it, Let thy name be called on thy handmaid to take me for wife, because thou art the redeemer; i.e., thou art the go'ēl, the kinsman, to whom the right of redemption belongs. Even to this present day, when a Jew marries a woman, he throws the skirt or end of his tallith over her, to signify that he has taken her under his protection."

He had already used the plural form of the word to her in chapter 2:12 – *"The LORD ... under whose wings you have come for refuge."* Now he realised she was looking for his redeeming wing to cover her and that, in effect, she was saying, "Be my kinsman-redeemer and marry me." She was a common gleaner, but she gave her double acknowledgement of what she was to him as a *"maidservant"* in verse 9, and it was met with his double acknowledgement of what she was to him as *"my daughter"* in verses 10 and 11. How enlightening this is for she didn't say, 'Your daughter', and he didn't say, 'My maidservant'! He conferred on her the honour and affection of a higher relationship, because he recognised her submission to God's law and her expectation of a godly man fulfilling it. He knew her background when he spoke with her in the field, but he knew her character and conduct when he spoke to her at his feet.

Lie down until morning

She had laboured in his field *"until evening"*[18] and lay at his feet *"until morning"*; action had been replaced by affection, and the public place had been replaced by the secret of his presence. She walked and sat and lay with him. Now her spirit was settled on his word *"until the morning,"* knowing that he would settle the matter of her redemption. Ours is, too, as we wait to see *"the Bright and Morning Star,"* and *"a morning without clouds."*[19] She had entered into his work in the field, and now she entered into his rest at his feet, but this wasn't an idle rest. Her rest was in his word, partly on his assurance of timing, but also in the content of his promise, *"I will do for you all that you request."*[20] This was a valued part of a threefold confirmation of their compatibility:

* Firstly, she sensed the assurance of a matching commitment that echoed what she said to Naomi in verse 5, *"All that you say to me I will do."*

* Secondly, he assured her of their matching character. He was a man of great "wealth," and he chose the same Hebrew word to describe her word when he said she was "virtuous."[21]

* Thirdly, they shared matching conduct for she knew he was "kindly" to her,[22] and he praised her for her "kindness" to him.[23]

In partnership, they symbolise the mutual fellowship of joy and blessing that co-exists between the Saviour and believers as they reflect the resemblance of the bride to the Bridegroom, the growth of the body with the Head, and the stability of the church with its Builder.

Bring ... and hold

From the first day until now, Boaz had much to give, and so it proved on that special morning when he told her, *"Bring the shawl that is on you and hold it."* She had kept it on in the cool of the night, but now what had surrounded her was about to be wrapped around the six measures of his blessing. It was worth holding, and, once filled, he laid it on her. On the face of it, this simply means he placed it on her as she prepared to carry it home, but the word *shiyth* can also suggest that he attired or dressed her with his gift. What a response to having dressed herself the previous night. Another consideration here is the impact this had on Naomi. For her to see how richly Boaz had provided for Ruth, and to know he had intentionally told her not to go *"empty-handed to your mother-in-law,"* would emphasise that he had no desire for her ever to know the emptiness she felt on her return from Moab. She had used the word *reykām* to describe the great void she felt in her life, and, by enriching her through Ruth, he ensured she would never feel such emptiness again. There is no word for "handed" in the Hebrew text, so he emphasised his care by using only the word *reykām*. Job was accused by one of his so-called comforters, *"You have sent widows away empty,"*[24] which was far from true. With a similar heart for the widow, Boaz made sure that Naomi shared in Ruth's fulness. It's all a wonderful picture of Israel being brought into the riches of God's blessing on Gentiles through the Christ, as we thought in chapter 1.

There is much in this that depicts the blessing we enjoy by having close communion with the Lord Jesus Christ. If we spend time with Him, we will have something to give to others. We shouldn't depend on getting fulfilment from working for Him when waiting on Him is such a blessing. Finding encouragement from what we do for Him is fine, but there's nothing more uplifting or rewarding than receiving satisfaction directly from Him. There is blessing to be found at his feet, and no one ever leaves poorer than when they came. Like Ruth, we will discover that we leave more behind than what we receive for it is *"of His fulness we have all received"*[25] and we will never exhaust *"the unsearchable riches of Christ."*[26]

In giving of His riches, He wants to attire us, so that the evidence of our witness is attributed to Him and not to ourselves. Ruth knew better than anyone that, even on her first day, what she took home wasn't all the result of her gleaning, even though she carried it home in the evening. But this day was completely different: what she carried was all of grace, and she took it home in the morning. No gleaner ever did that! She also took it home intact: none of it was lost on the way. What a way to go home! It's only as we think of our own blessings in Christ that we reflect what Ruth did by holding her shawl. She left him that morning as the lord of the harvest, but the next time she would see him would be as her bridegroom, and it's like this for us too. We work for the Lord of the harvest, and are waiting for our Bridegroom, whose word to each of us is, *"Only hold fast what you have until I come."*[27]

SOFTLY
"...and she came softly" (Ruth 3:7)

Softly, softly through the cornfield, past the heap of grain stacked high
To the spot where he was sleeping, softly, softly, Ruth drew nigh.
Washed and purified beforehand, sanctified with garments meet,
She came nearer, softly, softly, to lie down beside his feet.

Softly, softly to my Saviour as He hung on Calvary's tree,
With my load of sin and sorrow, which He bore instead of me.
One glad day I hastened softly at His pierced feet to fall,
And acknowledged Him as Sovereign, gladly yielding Him my all.

For the sake of my dear Saviour I would wash myself again,
And now sanctified completely I am free from every stain.
With His garments of salvation I am waiting, dignified,
To surrender all to Jesus, my Redeemer crucified.

Softly, softly, I would worship, at Your feet I humbly bow,
Blessed Bridegroom mould and fill me with Your Holy Spirit now.
(Danny Mawhinney)

10

UNTIL

"Now the two of them went until they came to Bethlehem" (Ruth 1:19).

"So she stayed close by the young women of Boaz, to glean until the end of barley harvest and wheat harvest; and she dwelt with her mother-in-law" (Ruth 2:23).

"Then she said, 'Sit still, my daughter, until you know how the matter will turn out; for the man will not rest until he has concluded the matter this day'" (Ruth 3:18).

* * *

God has glorious expectations locked into the word "until," and Scripture shows that it has been His marker for blessing from earliest days. Take Genesis 49:10, for example, where the coming of the Lord Jesus Christ is prophesied: *"The sceptre shall not depart from Judah, nor a lawgiver from between His feet, until Shiloh comes; and to Him shall be the obedience of the people."* In the glorious anticipation of the Incarnate Christ's coming back to reign on earth as the Messiah after the rapture of the church and the dark days of the great tribulation, the remnant of Israel will enjoy the fulfilment of God's purpose for them in this "until."

The theme is still about Him in the Passover of Exodus 12:6 when God told His people to take the lamb, *"Now you shall keep it until the fourteenth day of the same month. Then the whole assembly of the congregation of Israel shall kill it at twilight."* The One who prophesied the incarnation of Christ and His ultimate rule is now prophesying His crucifixion. He has moved our attention from the Man of the glory of Shiloh to the suffering Lamb of God. When we step in to Leviticus 23 and read through God's calendar of future events, He begins with the Passover and follows it with the Feast of Firstfruits. It's in this lovely portion of Israel's annual ceremony that God says to them in verse 14, *"You shall eat neither bread nor parched grain nor fresh grain until the same day that you have brought an offering to your God."* Now the "until" of the Incarnation, that became the "until" of the crucifixion, has become the "until" of the resurrection! These were deliberate and precise prophecies from God painted by Him in the landscape of Old Testament writings to portray what He will achieve in His Son.

The implications of the "until" are no less significant in the Book of Ruth. God is on the march. The three chapters that precede the marriage of Ruth to Boaz all end with an "until," and we can think of them as follows:

- at the end of chapter one, there's an anticipation of the place;
- at the end of chapter two, it's the anticipation of provision;
- at the end of chapter three, it's the anticipation of a partner.

Chapter 1 was a leaving process, chapter two was a learning process, and chapter three was a longing process. Coming to Bethlehem with Naomi meant all three for Ruth. They went on "until" they came to the place where God's providence, His purpose and His provision could be experienced, and their arrival coincided with the beginning of barley harvest. The timing was perfect for reaping the barley harvest began at Passover time in conjunction with the lamb that was from God for His people and the sheaf of the firstfruits that was from the people for God. How wonderfully He put the lamb and the sheaf together to symbolise that Jew and Gentile need the death and resurrection of Christ to unite them with Himself. We all went away from Him in Adam, and then Israel went away from Him as a nation; so Ruth represents us coming as lost sinners to our Redeemer, and Naomi is the picture of the remnant of Israel coming to receive His salvation. Both are vividly depicted in the treasury of Romans 11's goldmine, as we thought of them in our introduction in Chapter 1.

In 2007, Mahmoud Ahmadinejad the former president of Iran made an announcement that the USA, Great Britain and Israel will disappear from the world map. Well, he could be right on the first two, but he's definitely not right on the last. It's impossible, for her Redeemer has still to come, and the fulfilment of Naomi's return has still to be achieved in the deliverance of the remnant of Israel. Well might we borrow God's triumphant words from Isaiah 46:11, *"indeed I have spoken it; I will also bring it to pass. I have purposed it; I also will do it."*

Until the end

When Naomi said to Ruth, at the end of chapter 2, *"It is good, my daughter, that you go out with his young women, and that people do not meet you in any other field,"* Ruth knew that her place was set *"until the end of barley harvest and wheat harvest."* But the big difference was that she knew he had called it *"my harvest,"* so she was serving the lord of the harvest. What she didn't know, of course, was that although she was only a worker at the beginning of Boaz's barley harvest, she would be his wife before wheat harvest began.

These were two different crops. Unlike barley harvest, which began at Passover, Exodus 34:22 indicates that wheat harvest was associated with Pentecost: *"And you shall observe the Feast of Weeks, of the firstfruits of wheat harvest."* The Saviour's death on the cross was at Passover time and identified with His poverty, but Pentecost was associated with wheat harvest that points to His riches. If those who are *"born of the Spirit"*[1] also *"walk by the Spirit,"*[2] God will ensure that the sequel to Psalm 81:16 will be theirs. His word to His people was, *"He would have fed them also with the finest of wheat; and with honey from the rock I would have satisfied you."*

God's rich feeding always relates to fulness, fatness and sweetness, and in these lies the secret of being edified and satisfied. Just as coming to Christ guaranteed our leaving process, leaving our sinful and worldly ways, walking by the Spirit will guarantee our learning process. It's our anticipated provision, but we don't get it all at once. If the cross of Christ has brought a life-giving step, we will show it by allowing the Spirit of Christ to bring a life-changing walk. We met *"Christ our Passover"*[3] in our poverty, but we walk with Him in His riches *"until"* Christ is formed in us.[4] As we do, God will ensure that, *"He who has begun a good work in you will complete it until the day of Jesus Christ."*[5] He will do this if we adopt Paul's desire for Timothy, that he would *"keep the commandment, without spot, without reproach, until the appearing of our Lord Jesus Christ."*[6] Ruth served *"until,"* from *"the beginning"*[7] to *"the end,"*[8] and she knew the poverty of the barley and the fineness of the wheat by walking with the man who had said, *"my harvest."* Will we do that too?

Naomi had missed ten Passovers, so she couldn't claim that she had maintained fellowship with the lamb. The unmissable fact was she preferred bread! That's the lesson, and it teaches us we can't go away from God and keep having fellowship with Christ. Some claim they maintain a close relationship with the Lord Jesus, even while living in a sinful relationship with a partner. It's like living in Moab and claiming to being in fellowship with the lamb. As Jeremiah said, *"The heart is deceitful above all things,"*[9] and there are professing Christians who prove this to be true. Naomi knew there was only one remedy: she had to return to Bethlehem to be reconnected with God and with the lamb.

In God's goodness, there's a remedy for us, too: like lamenting Jeremiah, we need to say from deep conviction, *"Let us search out and examine our ways, and turn back to the LORD; let us lift our hearts and hands to God in heaven."*[10] He knows how real we are, and how unreal! That's why Jeremiah went on to say, *"You have covered Yourself with a cloud, that prayer should not pass through."* Christian, when you feel that the heavens are like brass[11] you can't also claim *"His heavens shall also drop dew."*[12] Evidence of His Spirit's presence never coexists with the absence of prayer contact with God, and the only answer is *"search ... examine ... turn."*

Naomi had missed the joy and satisfaction of these for ten years; but worse by far, the people of Israel have missed their sequel for two thousand years. At the darkest Passover time ever, they failed to see what Pilate, the Gentile governor saw. Having examined the Lamb of God, he reached his verdict and pronounced, *"I find no fault in Him."*[13] In response, they condemned Him and themselves, not only by saying, *"Crucify Him, crucify Him,"* but by adding, *"His blood be on us and on our children.*"[14]

Little did they know that by their permission the blood of the Passover Lamb would be shed in His crucifixion to fulfil Exodus 12, and that he would be cut off and lifted up in glorious resurrection as fulfilment of the wave sheaf in Leviticus 23. Oh, by what strange means we are caused to say to God, *"Surely the wrath of man shall praise You."*[15] In their blindness, they failed to reap the blessings that belong to the poverty of Christ depicted in *"the beginning of barley harvest"*; and were consigned to miss the further outpouring of His riches at Pentecost at *"the end of ... wheat harvest."* How triumphantly our Sheaf of the firstfruits went home! He has *"risen from the dead, and has become the firstfruits of those who have fallen asleep. For since by man came death, by Man also came the resurrection of the dead. For as in Adam all die, even so in Christ all shall be made alive. But each one in his own order: Christ the firstfruits, afterward those who are Christ's at His coming."* Harvest day is coming, and as we wait for it we can make truth out of what Eliphaz said to Job for believers will go home *"like sheaves gathered in season."*[16]

As each year passes, our prayer should be that we are growing more fully into conformity to Christ, and the greatest spiritual benefit we can be to each other is that we help one another to grow into the likeness of Christ. It's not merely helping what they do for Him, but assisting what they are for Him! Developing His character is what matters, but obtaining His depends on abstaining from our own. Paul made this link when he wrote, *"Therefore, having these promises, beloved, let us cleanse ourselves from all filthiness of the flesh and spirit, perfecting holiness in the fear of God."*[17] It takes a lot of honesty to answer Paul's question, *"For what man knows the things of a man except the spirit of the man which is in him?"*[18] There may be "things" in the recesses of our spirit that no one sees except the Lord, and we may need Him as the Carpenter to smooth our rough edges until He shapes us inwardly to His likeness.

But it's not wholly in the shaping of character; it's also in the developing of conduct. Blind spots exist, and each of us can say, 'I can be very tolerant of me.' That's easy. We can be adept at excusing ourselves, yet be intolerant of others. The spirit needs to change, so that our conduct changes. A lot rests on our spirit, including in how we conduct ourselves in gatherings of the Lord's people. At the beginning of Galatians 6, Paul urges churches to welcome back someone who has recovered from a fault, and he was looking for something deeper than an outward expression of acceptance. By saying, *"restore such a one in a spirit of gentleness,"* he emphasised that conduct and character go together, and he emphasised the solution in the final verse of his letter: *"Brethren, the grace of the Lord Jesus Christ be with your spirit."* Yes, we need the riches of His grace to be an ingredient of the finest of the wheat!

Until you know

Naomi's could sense that something was unfolding for Ruth, and this caused her good advice to continue at the end of chapter 3. *"Sit still, my daughter, until you know how the matter will turn out; for the man will not rest until he has concluded the matter this day."* Her word Sh*e*biy had strong implications that Ruth should feel settled there, as if she were married to the spot, and well might she for she had absolute trust in "the man." Does this depict the bond of trust there is between you and our Lord Jesus Christ, or is there a danger that you will be unsettled and not wait for Him to conclude whatever matter weighs on your mind?

The word *"until"* appears ten or eleven times in the Book of Ruth, depending upon which English version you read, and we find it twice in this verse. It's as if the whole book hangs on these *"untils."* They were deep experiences for her, and the two we are now looking at speak to us, not of the living process or learning process, but of the longing process that had come into her heart. She knew that God had made provision in His Law[19] for a close relative of her husband to marry her, and she quietly rested on this. Did that mean sitting idle and doing nothing? No, for the second *"until"* tells us that she was fully prepared to show that her definition of sitting still didn't mean an attitude of indolence, but one of dependence. It was no haphazard longing, and neither is ours. Those who belong to *"the Man Christ Jesus"*[20] are perfectly settled and waiting, and will continue to do so *"until the redemption of the purchased possession."*[21]

Far greater than Ruth's, our waiting time will be worth it. If she could be content to *"sit still,"* believing that her *"until"* would pass and, ultimately, she would stand at his side, how much more should we? God assures us in His Word that we have the certainty of Christ's return, and this caused James to say, *"Therefore be patient, brethren, until the coming of the Lord."* Ruth lived in the presence and power of each *"until,"* but believers in our Lord Jesus Christ live in the promise of each "until" that God has given us. Today, like Ruth, we "sit still," settled in the sure hope of His coming, but soon we also shall stand as a bride at the side of our Bridegroom: *"For in just a little while, He who is coming will come and will not delay."*[22] He *"was offered once to bear the sins of many. To those who eagerly wait for Him He will appear a second time, apart from sin, for salvation."*[23]

Soon the watching will be over,
And the waiting time be past,
Earthly praying will be ended;
We shall meet our Lord at last.
(Miss I. Hickling)

My heart can sing when I pause to remember
A heartache here is but a stepping stone
Along a trail that's winding always upward,
This troubled world is not my final home.

But until then my heart will go on singing,
Until then with joy I'll carry on,
Until the day my eyes behold the city,
Until the day God calls me home.

(Stuart Hamblen)

11

BOAZ THE BRIDEGROOM

"Now it is true that I am a close relative; however, there is a relative closer than I" (Ruth 3:12).

Now Boaz went up to the gate and sat down there; and behold, the close relative of whom Boaz had spoken came by. So Boaz said, "Come aside, friend, sit down here." So he came aside and sat down. And he took ten men of the elders of the city, and said, "Sit down here." So they sat down. Then he said to the close relative, "Naomi, who has come back from the country of Moab, sold the piece of land which belonged to our brother Elimelech. And I thought to inform you, saying, 'Buy it back in the presence of the inhabitants and the elders of my people. If you will redeem it, redeem it; but if you will not redeem it, then tell me, that I may know; for there is no one but you to redeem it, and I am next after you.'" And he said, "I will redeem it."

Then Boaz said, "On the day you buy the field from the hand of Naomi, you must also buy it from Ruth the Moabitess, the wife of the dead, to perpetuate the name of the dead through his inheritance." And the close relative said, "I cannot redeem it for myself, lest I ruin my own inheritance. You redeem my right of redemption for yourself, for I cannot redeem it."

Now this was the custom in former times in Israel concerning redeeming and exchanging, to confirm anything: one man took off his sandal and gave it to the other, and this was a confirmation in Israel. Therefore the close relative said to Boaz, "Buy it for yourself." So he took off his sandal. And Boaz said to the elders and all the people, "You are witnesses this day that I have bought all that was Elimelech's, and all that was Chilion's and Mahlon's, from the hand of Naomi.

Moreover, Ruth the Moabitess, the widow of Mahlon, I have acquired as my wife, to perpetuate the name of the dead through his inheritance, that the name of the dead may not be cut off from among his brethren and from his position at the gate. You are witnesses this day" (Ruth 4:1-10).

* * *

It was in the main store in Madras, South India, while a package was being wrapped for me, a member of staff at another counter was reading a small book. He was so engrossed that he didn't know he was being watched. Evidently, he was reading some Hindu scriptures for, as he turned each page, he lifted the book to his lips and kissed it, and the thought flashed through my mind: "I wish I loved my Bible as much as that man appears to love his book."

Ruth's story is one good reason for loving God's Word for it is a treasure within a treasury, and reflects a characteristic harmony that has been given by its Inspirer. It opens without a king[1] and closes with a king; it begins with death, and it ends in birth; it starts with division, and finishes in union. We have already thought of how chapter 1 opens with famine and ends with plenty; chapter 2 starts with barley harvest and finishes with wheat harvest; chapter 3 opens with Boaz at rest and concludes with Ruth at rest. In that chapter, she went down. Chapter

4 says, *"Boaz went up."* There's something about the way God does things that makes us stand in awe and recognise that, no matter who the author is on earth, His hand is behind the penmanship. It would be strange if chapter 4 were any different, and it's not, for it begins with ten witnesses and ends with ten generations. The amazing balance is everywhere!

Verse 1 of chapter 4 doesn't tell us that *"Boaz went up"* simply to stand as a contrast to what we read in chapter 3 that *"she went down."* There's more to it than that. The world *'ālāh* means to ascend, but is very closely associated to the word *'ōlāh* which refers to the burnt offering in Leviticus. The ascending of the burnt offering was more than upward; it was Godward, and wholly for God. This captures the deeper intention in the heart and mind of Boaz as he went up. Ten other men went up to the gate that morning, but only Boaz went up for God, yet he wasn't aware that he was going up to fulfil a key part of the purpose of God. Yes, he knew that he was going up to honour the provision made in the law for a redeemer, but he had no idea that God saw his going up as a step toward fulfilling His provision of the Redeemer under grace.

In Exodus 24, we are told four times that Moses *"went up,"* and chapter 19:3 says, *"Moses went up to God."* The people should have been so gripped by the sight of the ascending, receding figure, and every heart should have been acknowledging, "He's going up for me." Ruth could have said the same, and, thankfully, so can we. Luke 2 adds its own remarkable commentary of how the twelve-year-old Jesus *"went up"* to Jerusalem with His parents for the Passover. What a scene! The Lamb, *"Christ, our Passover"*[2] was there! But a greater day was coming for which *"He went on,"*[3] then *"He, bearing His cross, went out,"*[4] and three days later *"He went up."*[5] It was the greatest going up of all, for the One who had offered Himself on the cross was the true ascending Offering going home.

The Purpose of the Gate

The gate was a place of discussion and debate, where decisions were made, and Boaz knew that local matters of justice and judgment would be settled there, including important issues like redemption. The practice was steeped in history, the first scriptural example being Sodom in the opening verse of Genesis 19, but its spiritual connotation is presented in chapter 28:17 where Jacob woke from his dream at Bethel and announced, *"How awesome is this place! This is none other than the house of God, and this is the gate of heaven!"* Apart from being the place of access, it also implies a place of divine authority that calls for submission to its claims and control, and a place of opportunity. It was there that Jacob took his stone pillow and upended it as a pillar.

This imagery is captured in 1 Timothy 3:15 for present-day application to disciples walking together and having their behaviour governed *"in the house of God, which is the church of the living God, the pillar and ground of the truth."* This is made clear in the previous verses, which apply to godly conditions being applied in very practical ways in our homes and in His house. Those who love Jesus *"the door"*[6] as their access to salvation shouldn't struggle to comply with subjection at "the gate" for service.

Job also spoke of his ministry at the gate,[7] and it still does our hearts good to sense the range of pastoral care that should be available at "the gate." It wasn't just a men's meeting, this was a place where whatever was relevant to everyone and everything was considered. Job's list of those present included young men, the aged, princes and nobles, and he made an impact on the poor, the fatherless, the widow, the blind, and the lame. He could do all that at the gate. He was the ideal role model for the ideal overseers' meeting!

Another telling example comes from the occasion when Jeremiah was left to sink in the dungeon and Ebed-Melech pleaded with the king who *"was sitting at the Gate of Benjamin."*[8] This may seem an unimportant detail until we recall that when Benjamin was born his mother, Rachel, wanted to call him Ben-Oni: son of my sorrow. If Rachel's will had been carried out, Ebed-Melech would have gone to see the king at the Gate of Ben-Oni, the son of my sorrow, but Jacob's intervention meant he went to the Gate of the son of the right hand, the place of victory and triumph.

Boaz came to the gate believing it was a place of divine ministry. It wasn't a talking shop, but a place where the voice of God was heard and where His confirmation was given through what was discussed and decided. Once there, he *"sat down"* to wait for the close relative (from *yāshab*), just as Ruth was able to *"sit still"* (also from *yāshab*) to wait for him to settle his right to redeem:

> *"According to the principle of levirate marriage, the next brother (or, as we note later, kinsman) was expected to marry the childless widow of his deceased brother. The first child of the second marriage was accounted to the deceased brother, and that child carried on the family name and inherited the property as if he had been the child of the deceased man"* (The Wycliffe Bible Commentary).

Boaz's call to him was probably from familiarity for, although some versions translate it as *"Come, my friend"* or *"Come over here, my friend,"* his phrase, *pᵉloniy 'almoniy*, can mean *"such a one"* (JND), *"such and such,"*[9] or *"so and so."* With this low-key welcome, Boaz ensured there was neither tension nor rivalry and gave him the opportunity, but not the obligation, to redeem the land and Ruth.

There was no conflict or animosity between them, just as there's none between the law and grace. The law is holy, spiritual, righteous and good,[10] and so is grace for they both came from the heart of God. But the law had limitations and so did the close relative with whom Boaz spoke. Initially, the man said, *"I will redeem it,"* but when he discovered that he also had to redeem Ruth his answer became, *"I cannot redeem it for myself, lest I ruin my own inheritance."* The Keil & Delitzsch Commentary explains this:

> *"The redemption would cost money, since the yearly produce of the field would have to be paid for up to the year of Jubilee. Now, if he acquired the field by redemption as his own property, he would have increased by so much his own possessions. But if he should marry Ruth, the field so redeemed would belong to the son whom he would beget through her, and he would therefore have parted with the money that he had paid for the redemption merely for the son of Ruth, so that he would have withdrawn a certain amount of capital from his own possession, and to that extent have detracted from its worth."*

He wasn't prepared for this, so Boaz triumphed in grace.

Ten men of the elders of the city

God sometimes works with tens. Chapter 1 speaks about ten years; chapter 4 about ten witnesses. The number often is symbolic of responsibility and irresponsibility. For example, going away from

Bethlehem for ten years was irresponsible, but bringing ten men was responsible. Ten commandments were given In Exodus 20 to govern the lives of men and women on earth and to show them the difference between the irresponsible and the responsible. The ten men at the gate were there to verify the agreement made by Boaz and the other man, and they probably formed a quorum, just as a minyan is adopted among present-day Jews. This is not the only time that God used witnesses. The most outstanding example is in Romans 8 in the matter of adoption.

"It is only when we understand how serious and complicated a step Roman adoption was that we really understand the depth of meaning in this passage. Roman adoption was always rendered more serious and more difficult by the *patria potestas*. The *patria potestas* was the father's power over his family; that power was absolute; it was actually the absolute power of disposal and control, and in the early days it was actually the power of life and death. In regard to his father a Roman son never came of age. No matter how old he was, he was still under the *patria potestas*, in the absolute possession, and under the absolute control, of his father. Obviously this made adoption into another family a very difficult and a very serious step. In adoption a person had to pass from one *patria potestas* to another. He had to pass out of the possession and control of one father into the equally absolute possession and control of another. There were two steps.

The first was known as *mancipatio*, and it was carried out by a symbolic sale in which copper and scales were symbolically used. Three times the symbolism of sale was carried out. Twice the father symbolically sold his son, and twice he bought him back; and the third time he did not buy him back, and thus the *patria potestas* was held to be broken. After the sale there was a ceremony called *vindicatio*. The adopting father went to the *praetor*, one of the Roman magistrates, and presented a legal case for the transference of the person to be adopted into his *patria potestas*. When all this was completed then the adoption was complete. Clearly this was a serious and impressive step. But it was the consequences of adoption which are most significant for the picture that is in Paul's mind. There were four main consequences.

1. The adopted person lost all rights in his old family, and gained all the rights of a fully legitimate son in his new family. In the most literal sense, and in the most binding legal way, he got a new father.
2. It followed that he became an heir to his new father's estate. Even if other sons were afterwards born, who were real blood relations, it did not affect his rights. He was inalienably co-heir with them.
3. In law, the old life of the adopted person was completely wiped out. For instance, legally all debts were cancelled; they were wiped out as if they had never been. The adopted person was regarded as a new person entering into a new life with which the past had nothing to do.
4. In the eyes of the law the adopted person was literally and absolutely the son of his new father...

He uses still another picture from Roman adoption. He says that God's Spirit witnesses with our spirit that we really are children of God. The adoption process was carried out in the presence of seven witnesses. Now, suppose the adopting father died, and then suppose that there was some dispute about the right of the adopted son to inherit, one or more of the seven witnesses stepped forward and swore that the adoption was genuine and true. Thus the right of the inheritance was guaranteed and he entered into his inheritance. So Paul is saying, it is the Holy Spirit Himself who is the witness to our adoption into the family of God ...

It was Paul's picture that when a man became a Christian he entered into the very family of God. He did nothing to earn it; he did nothing to deserve it; God, the great Father in His amazing love and mercy, has taken the lost, helpless, poverty-stricken, debt-laden sinner and adopted him into His own family, so that the debts are cancelled and the unearned love and glory inherited." (William Barclay on Romans).

Boaz prefigured the Lord Jesus Christ in different ways throughout this process. Firstly, by fulfilling the requirements of the law, he pointed forward to the One who would *"exalt the law and make it honorable."*[11] Secondly, he was willing to have Ruth as his bride within his inheritance, and we see this perfectly expressed in Ephesians 1:18-19, *"that you may know what is the hope of His calling, what are the riches of the glory of His inheritance in the saints, and what is the exceeding greatness of His power toward us who believe."* The cross of our Redeemer has guaranteed "His hope ... His inheritance ... and ... His power" for Himself, while guaranteeing *"our hope,"*[12] *"our inheritance,"*[13] and *"power"* for us.[14] Through the blood of His cross our Redeemer has paid the full price to secure an inheritance for Himself and for every believer. All the wealth of His goodness, grace and glory are ours; and we are *"heirs of God and joint heirs with Christ."*[15] Sir John Bowring, former governor of Hong Kong put it well when he said:

> In the cross of Christ I glory,
> Tow'ring o'er the wrecks of time;
> All the light of sacred story
> Gathers round its head sublime.

The house of him who had his sandal removed

On hearing the outcome of the discussion between Boaz and the other relative, Ruth could have exercised her right to go up to the gate to confront the unwilling redeemer, but she didn't. She preferred to "sit still" by faith and, with Naomi's help, decided she didn't need to react as she was entitled by the law to disgrace him from head to foot:

"But if the man does not want to take his brother's wife, then let his brother's wife go up to the gate to the elders, and say, 'My husband's brother refuses to raise up a name to his brother in Israel; he will not perform the duty of my husband's brother.' Then the elders of his city shall call him and speak to him. But if he stands firm and says, 'I do not want to take her,' then his brother's wife shall come to him in the presence of the elders, remove his sandal from his foot, spit in his face, and answer and say, 'So shall it be done to the man who will not build up his brother's house.'"

Under this provision, other disappointed women would have called for a threefold face-to-face response, but Ruth had no desire to go up to the gate to speak her mind, to spit in his face or pull off his sandal. She hadn't come to Bethlehem looking for law, but for grace, and grace didn't retaliate. Instead, she rested through faith on what God would provide by grace. What a lovely picture she gave of sinners hearing God's word in Ephesians 2:8 – *"For by grace you have been saved through faith, and that not of yourselves, it is the gift of God."* The truth is that she didn't need to be there for the man suddenly bent down and took off his sandal and handed it to Boaz. It literally means that he plucked it off, as swiftly as a soldier unsheathing his sword.[16] It was a practice in Israel that, when a man decided that a property was not a place where he wanted to set his foot, he would take off his sandal as an indication of surrendering his right, of renouncing his claim, and of voluntarily losing his title.

The man who forfeited his right to Boaz is like the law yielding to the greater claims of grace, not that he typified a weak law, but rather a law that was weak through the flesh. In this, he proves Romans 8:3 and 4, *"For what the law could not do in that it was weak through the flesh, God did by sending His own Son in the likeness of sinful flesh, on account of sin: He condemned sin in the flesh, that the righteous requirement of the law might be fulfilled in us who do not walk according to the flesh but according to the Spirit."* God's law never retaliates against His grace, like those who are weak through the flesh, but acknowledges its limitations and surrenders. Nor was it the law that abused Him with the unclean insult of spitting in His face,[17] but ungodly Jews who broke their own law in the weakness of their own flesh. The contrast could hardly be greater: in grace, Ruth never spat on an unwilling redeemer's face, yet those who were weak through the flesh spat on the willing Redeemer's face!

As we triumph in our Saviour's rightful claim on His redeemed, it's good that we ask if our lives prove that previous claimants have lost their claim. Have all our rights been fully surrendered to Christ? Are we the kind of people who have plucked off our sandal or do we resemble those whose sandals are firmly stuck to their feet like a sword wedged in its scabbard? Figuratively speaking, our sandal can be in only one of two places: on our feet or in His hand. Which will it be? Will we surrender our right to self by saying, *"it is no longer I who live, but Christ lives in me"*?[18] Will we forsake our right to the world, and its right to us, since our boast is *"in the cross of our Lord Jesus Christ, by whom the world has been crucified to me, and I to the world"*?[19] And will we show that the adversary's rights have been severed, because we have turned *"from darkness to light, and from the power of Satan to God"*?[20]

As those who are waiting to meet our Redeemer, let's encourage one another to be men and women who have yielded our rights to Him. It should be our custom[21] to surrender, but have we given Him our sandal?

I have acquired as my wife

Boaz was a man of great wealth, yet through redemption he chose not to be bride-less, and by obtaining his bride he anticipated *"that the name of the dead may not be cut off from among his brethren."* This was his thoughtful, considerate retrospective look – honouring the names of Elimelech, Chilion and Mahlon – yet the prospective look that God had was all unknown to him, that the Name above all names ultimately would come from the line of Ruth, his bride. But he was bride-less no more, and neither is our Lord Jesus Christ. Through the seal of His Redemption, He has purchased His bride and we can never be lost!

As chapter 4 nears its end, Naomi took Ruth's newborn infant, Obed the servant, and laid him on her bosom. She took him to her heart. Isn't that the implication? She held him at the centre of her affections. Oh, there was no sign of Marah now! No, it was with joy she became his "nurse," in her language the word *'omeneth* belongs to *'āman*, as if she were saying 'Amen' to the wonder of God's purpose. Praise God, the day is coming when Israel will say it too. At last, they will take their Messiah to heart and rejoice that His goodness and grace have brought them into greater riches than they ever knew under law.

The day when Jesus stood alone
And felt the hearts of men like stone,
And knew He came but to atone
That day "He held His peace."

They witnessed falsely to His word,
They bound Him with a cruel cord,
And mockingly proclaimed Him Lord;
"But Jesus held His peace."

They spat upon Him in the face,
They dragged Him on from place to place,
They heaped upon Him all disgrace;
"But Jesus held His peace."

My friend, have you for far much less,
With rage, which you called righteousness,
Resented slights with great distress?
Your Saviour "held His peace."
(L.S.P.)[22]

12

NOT LEFT WITHOUT A REDEEMER

"Then the women said to Naomi, "Blessed be the LORD, who has not left you this day without a redeemer, and may his name be renowned in Israel" (Ruth 4:14 ESV).

* * *

We thank God for verses that leap out from the page of Scripture and fix themselves in our minds, and then allow us to begin the process of dividing them into segments, like peeling an orange and squeezing as much juice from them as possible. Ruth 4:14 is such a verse, as long as we honour its place in its context.

In earlier days, while involved with carpet manufacturing something glinted in the pile of a sample and caught my eye. To my surprise, it was a diamond. Wondering whether it was of any value, I went to a nearby jeweller to hear his opinion. "Yes," he said, "it's a valuable diamond, but it would be of more value in its setting." I have never forgotten that, because it's equally applicable when we come to verses of Scripture. No matter what verse it is from which we derive particular pleasure, as soon as we re-evaluate it in its setting we automatically discover a resonance it never had on its own that radiates a spectrum of divine light borrowed from its surroundings in God's Word.

It's like this with the Lord's call in Matthew 11:28, isn't it? *"Come unto Me, all you who labour and are heavy laden, and I will give you rest."* What a marvellous verse! Many have responded to His words and tucked them away in their hearts to do them good for a lifetime, but put them in their setting and we will discover how much they increase in value. Listen to the wider range of His message, and notice how He called on God before calling on men: an upward plea before the outward:

"I thank You, Father, Lord of heaven and earth, that You have hidden these things from the wise and prudent and have revealed them to babes. Even so, Father, for so it seemed good in Your sight. All these things have been delivered to Me by my Father, and no one knows the Son except the Father. Nor does anyone know the Father except the Son, and the one to whom the Son wills to reveal Him."

It's then He called, *"Come to Me."* Now we can see how the context enhances the content of His call, as the attributes of the Caller give reasons for a response from the called. First of all, there's His own relationship with God as His Father. Secondly, He showed the relevance of His call to everyday folk who wouldn't see themselves as being included in *"the wise and prudent,"* and how this expresses the Father's will. Thirdly, as Speaker, He confirmed His co-equality with God and helped those to whom He spoke to sense that He alone has the authority to reveal the Father and call them into a true relationship with Him. The purpose of God had been safely confined to the hands of Him whom He sent, and they can be safely in them, too, by coming. By emphasising what is God-centred and Christ-centred His man-centred words have greater appeal, and all this lies behind verse 28. Suddenly, the diamond sparkles in a way it never did on its own, because of the greater breadth and depth of what the Lord Jesus was saying.

It's the same with Hebrews 13 verse 8: *"Jesus Christ is the same yesterday, today, and forever."* This is another tremendous verse, yet it also sparkles in a way that it doesn't when isolated from the surrounding text. Having commended the stability of leaders who ministered the unchanging Word of God in verse 7, the contrast is made in verse 9 with a warning against being carried along by many shades of teaching that are foreign to the Word. The secret of true spiritual stability is found in being stabilised by grace, which is only to be found in the changeless Jesus of verse 8. Once again, the verse is made to sparkle in its setting between the verses on either side.

The whole Book of Ruth is like this; and we do well to see chapter 4:14, not only in the context of the Book of Ruth itself, but in its Bible-wide setting. This will help us to see how the gleam of all Scripture shines into it through its setting, so that the facets of the diamond radiate with refracted light that draws us even more fully to the Saviour than the single verse does on its own. *"Blessed be the LORD, who has not left you this day without a redeemer,"* is a word from the Lord that we can take with us and rejoice in forever. But let's explore it through the avenue of the book's four chapters, and then see the whole book in the overall setting of its Bible-wide context of God's revelation. When we do this, we will recognise that it has a consistent representation of the gospel, and a consistent presentation of God that draws us in even more closely than the single verse did. In matchless wisdom, God is proving the interdependence of all Scripture, which we thought about at the beginning of Chapter 1's introduction, and opening up the wider foreshadowing of His coming Redeemer and the wonder of His redemption.

In Exodus 12, the blood-stained doorways of God's people meant that they would open their doors in the morning and go forward in the liberty and victory of the lamb and never go back. Prior to that, God had said very clearly in Exodus 8:23, *"I will make a difference between My people and your* [Pharaoh's] *people,"* and He didn't simply mean that there would be a division between them. It was much more than a distinction or a line of demarcation, He was announcing their deliverance by assuring them He had *"set redemption"* (RV margin). To begin with, this meant they were saved from plagues that caused harm and death in Egypt, including a darkness that brought everything to a standstill in their homes. *"But all the children of Israel had light in their dwellings."*[1]

Finally, in the Passover, God's people could testify, *"He struck the Egyptians and delivered our households"*[2]; and they mourned, *"for there was not a house where there was not one dead."*[3] The Passover brought light and life: similarly, before writing about *"The Lamb of God who takes away the sin of the world,"*[4] John said of Him, *"In Him was life, and the life was the light of men."*[5] He had come that God might set redemption through His blood and make a division between believer and unbeliever, and an eternal distinction between those who are saved and those who are lost.

God drew a definite line at Calvary, as did David when he came to the Vale of Elah, the valley of the tree, and stood at Ephes Dammim, which literally means the boundary of bloodshed. At such a significant landmark, David defeated Goliath to prefigure his greater Son who went to Calvary's tree to set His own boundary of bloodshed and *"destroy him who had the power of death, that is the devil."*[6] This is the great triumph of the gospel of Christ: through repentance and conversion we cross the boundary line that He set in His death and find refuge in His redemption.

When you think of the realm of great Bible events, there are three in particular that are given unique divine approval. The first is in the book of Genesis in the time of the flood when God showed His displeasure in the catastrophe that took place, yet demonstrated His grace at the same time in calling eight souls into the ark to know His safekeeping and blessing. It took the buffeting of the deluge for them, just as Christ endured the buffeting of the cross for us while God's waves and billows swept over Him. In the deepest way of all, He faced the full blast described in Psalm 42:7, *"All Your waves and billows have gone over me,"* and Psalm 88:7, *"Your wrath lies heavy upon me, and You have afflicted me with all Your waves."* How grateful we are that it was in that storm He made peace for us through the blood of His cross.[7]

In Genesis, the ark was the means of a new beginning with these eight people – Noah and his wife, their three sons and their wives – just as in the Gospels God gave a greater new beginning through another eight – Zacharias, Elizabeth, and John the Baptist; Mary, Joseph and Jesus; Simeon and Anna.

Between these two great times of divine intervention, we find the momentous story of Ruth and the accompanying similarity of bringing her centre stage among eight named characters: Elimelech, Naomi, Mahlon and Chilion, Orpah and Ruth, Boaz and Obed. So there are three outstanding God-given events:

- In Genesis, a new beginning through judgment;
- In Ruth, a new beginning through a Gentile;
- In the gospel, a new beginning through Jesus.

– and the number eight is consistently associated with a new beginning in each one, just as we also would find if we began to explore scriptures that speak about the eighth day.

Spiritual decline always begins by losing sight of God; and there's something very precious about keeping our eyes on Him. For the right reasons, His eyes are in every place, but it's not such a good thing when ours do the same for the wrong reasons! We want our eyes to be on Him and the evidence of Elimelech and Naomi and their boys having lost sight of God was seen when they went to dwell in the land of Moab. Some Bible versions say they went to "sojourn," which means they went there to be inhabitants, and they "remained" or became committed to it. It's as if they transferred their citizenship and, declining what was His, walked away from Him.

When we look at the journey Ruth took toward Bethlehem, she stands in stark contrast to her husband and in-laws in the journey they took away from it. Her vision was very God-centred, while theirs was self-centred, and we need to ask ourselves which of these two journeys we are on. Our Bibles also tell the story of another young woman, Esther, who lived in a climate where God wasn't mentioned, and it was in that environment she courted the attention of a wealthy Gentile. Ruth's experience was so different: God was mentioned more than twenty times; recognised as Jehovah, Elohim and Shaddai, and it was in that climate she prepared to marry a wealthy Jew.

There's a balance going on in the Book of Ruth that indicates something of the majestic workings of God, and we can see this as Ruth is being drawn towards Bethlehem in the company of her mother-in-law. On the outward journey away from God there were four; on the homeward journey, Naomi was the only one left. It's as if there was only a remnant coming home, and isn't this a picture of how it's going to be at the last? Zechariah tells us about Jerusalem in chapter 14:2 that, *"Half of the city shall go into captivity, but the remnant of the people shall not be cut off from the city."* Immediately, he adds, *"Then the LORD will go forth."*

How tragic that half will give up just before He arrives, and the other half wonderfully delivered by their Messiah-Redeemer when He comes to make Himself known on the earth. There are divisions in Ruth's story, too, for we discover two women in the first chapter, one of one whom reneged and couldn't be redeemed; and in the last chapter we meet two men, one of whom reneged and couldn't be the redeemer. Reading these tragedies highlights the present possibility of beloved fellow-believers who lose heart and give up when they would be blessed by going on. How real the Lord's question is, and how heart-searching, *"Do you also want to go away?"*[8]

Ruth was bound to have heard of the land of Israel because there were times when the people of Moab must have spoken to one another about what was going on in Israel, not least in the days of Ehud who slew their king. The people of Moab must have been impacted in a way that would have its knock-on effect on young women like Ruth. After all, the God of Israel had not only made Himself known, He had exposed the impotence of their gods.

During the Normandy Landings in 1944, a young soldier in one of the vessels found his mind being lifted from the battle as the words of this poem formulated in his mind.

> He has fixed the set proportion of the ocean and the land
> According to the detail of His plan;
> He has measured out the waters in the hollow of His hand

And meted out the heaven with a span.

But although that arm is power in the infinite expanse,
That same unerring hand is in control
To determine and to govern in my every circumstance –
And to claim supreme submission in my soul.
(R.G. Fear)

Naomi had a very different thought in mind as she anticipated arriving in Bethlehem and spoke about that omnipotent hand having *"gone out against her."* I wonder where we are with the hand of our omnipotent God. Can you say like Ezra, *"I was encouraged, as the hand of the LORD my God was upon me,"*[9] and tell others like Nehemiah, *"And I told them of the hand of my God which had been good upon me"*?[10] Are you assured, as they were, of His approving and commending hand; or do you feel like Naomi that His disapproving and condemning hand is against you? Ruth must have felt the haunting, pathetic echo of these words – *"gone out against"* – yet it was at her mother-in-law's side she was about to discover that same unerring hand was in control to determine and to govern in her every circumstance, and to claim supreme submission in her soul.

This is the secret of knowing the hand that reaches and touches and confers His blessing. Naomi's return was one of mixed feelings, and maybe you can relate to her because of some regret in your life. Ruth was different. She was an outstanding example of someone who wholeheartedly and unreservedly says, *"The blessing of the LORD makes one rich, and He adds no sorrow with it."*[11] And we can say it, too, and add, *"This I know, because God is for me."*[12]

If we were studying Paul's letter to the Romans, we would enjoy the privilege of thinking about the glory of God. Were we considering the letter to the Hebrews, we would be led into the majesty of His greatness. Moving forward and reading Peter's first letter, we would be treated to his rich appreciation of His grace. Ruth's little book makes no mention of His glory, nor is there any reference to His greatness, but, like Peter, grace is everywhere. The marvel is, that as we absorb the proofs of kindness and favour in its four chapters, we sense that the glory of God and greatness of God are stamped on each one for they depict something so grand in its great and glorious message of redemption.

Orpah came so near to it, and turned back. Leaving home, as Ruth did, she came to a point in the journey where Naomi's appeal became her way of escape; the way to God and freedom apparently lost forever. Whatever seed may have been sown, at last bore no fruit. If we borrow the imagery of the parable of the sower, Orpah was like those who answer to the wayside, the stony places or among thorns.[13] As she accompanied Naomi and Ruth, she may have looked like a ripening stalk, but there was no grain and she returned to her ungodly place not harvested.

Naomi knew the route as she retraced her steps. She had travelled it ten years earlier, and memories must have flooded back as she recalled going in the opposite direction with her husband and sons. The northern route would have taken them past Jericho, the place of the first victory of faith that the people of God ever knew in the land, then across the Jordan into the land of Moab. Ultimately, on its plains, they would be in the region where God told Moses to speak to the children of Israel about crossing over the Jordan.[14] It was a day when, as Hebrews, they fulfilled the root meaning of their name, which includes the thought of crossing over. Sadly, Elimelech and family had crossed over in the opposite direction. They had left, not entered. They had gone out, not come in. They displeased God, not pleased Him. Now, ten years later,

Naomi was going in the right direction: crossing over – a Hebrew in the land, but motivated by looking for grain.

Ruth was at her side, drawn by a power far greater than Naomi, and she had a longing in her heart: she was looking for grace. In chapter 1, she was a widow; in chapter 2, a worker; in chapter 3, she was waiting at her redeemer's feet; and in chapter 4, she was a wife. She had known what it was to be a foreigner; she knew what it was to be in the field; she has known what it was to be at Boaz's feet, but she would never be satisfied until at last she knew what it was to be in his family. She met him as proprietor in chapter 2, as lord of the harvest in chapter 3, and finally as her redeemer and bridegroom in chapter 4. What tremendous progress, and what an example she is of the journey we have made to our Redeemer!

"My Redeemer, oh what beauties in that lovely name appear
None but Jesus in his glory shall the honoured title wear."

Yes, He wears it, and He shares it with us. How thankful we are that the Spirit of God brings this message to us: *"Blessed be the LORD, who has not left you this day without a Redeemer."* Can you imagine being without your Redeemer? He is the personification of love, and He alone causes us to say that He is the *"Son of God who loved me and gave Himself for me."*[15] We look at the book of Ruth and call it a love story, but the word "love" appears only once, and we find it in chapter 4:15. It's not the love of God, it's not the love of Ruth for Boaz or his for her, it's her love for Naomi, yet the whole story is one of God's redeeming love, and the love of a redeemer and his bride. How wonderfully it all points to our Redeemer of whom Paul says, *"Christ also loved the church and gave Himself for her."*[16]

With its close association to Calvary's incomparable demonstration of the Saviour's love, we may find it intriguing that the word "love" doesn't appear at all in the Acts of the Apostles, yet the evidence of love is on every page. Similarly, the letter to the Hebrews make no mention of light, yet the One who is the brightness of God's glory in chapter 1:3 shines right through its thirteen chapters. When we reach the end of the book of the Acts, we won't find the word "disciple" in the remaining twenty-two books of the Bible, yet the theme of all the letters is discipleship.

Yes, our verse is like a diamond in the cameo we thought of in the opening paragraph of our introduction, but now it's ablaze with colour as it reflects the valuable theme of redemption that's traced in the little book of Ruth. More than that, all the great truths of the gospel associated with redemption in the Epistle to the Romans come with dazzling power and shine their light into it, and so does the light of the Person who is the brightness of God's glory in Hebrews. Everything combines to assure Jew and Gentile alike that God has provided a Redeemer. Ruth's short message reminds us that, just as Naomi brought her to God and His land, so the law is our tutor to bring us as Gentiles to Christ.[17]

She also points us in the direction of seeing that, as Naomi was brought into the joy of Ruth's redeemer, so also the Jewish nation will be brought to know Christ as their Redeemer when He comes to Zion.[18] The writer to the Hebrews adds to this by saying, *"God having provided some better thing for us, that apart from us they should not be made perfect."*[19] At last, they will be broken in heart before the Man of the cross, and He will acknowledge their return by saying, *"they will look on Me whom they pierced."*[20]

Ruth helped Naomi and Naomi helped Ruth for the Jew brought a message to the Gentile, and through the Gentile God had a message for the Jew. What a story for through it we see the Lord Jesus as the answer to:

- the lamb of Passover at the time of the barley harvest;[21]
- the wave sheaf for the day of his resurrection;[22]
- the handful of parched corn;[23]
- the Bethlehemite;[24]
- Lord of the harvest;[25]
- the Redeemer;[26]
- the Beloved.[27]

– and, more than any, we are able to say, *"Blessed be the LORD, who has not left us this day without a Redeemer."*

Oh, my Redeemer, how can I be silent
When Thou art bestowing such blessings on me?
Surely Thy mercy has followed me ever,
My heart is o'erflowing, I'm happy in Thee.

Safe in Thy watch-care no evil can harm me,
Thou chargest Thine angels my guardians to be;
And so I go onward, upheld and protected,
Believing Thy promise and trusting in Thee.

Oh, my Redeemer, how can I be silent
When Thou art so precious, Thy presence so near?
I will exalt Thee, and tell of Thy goodness,
My voice in the morning, O Lord, thou shalt hear.

I will exalt Thee, for Thou art my Saviour,
Thy word is a light and a lamp unto me.
And so I go onward through shadow and sunshine,
Believing Thy promise and trusting in Thee.
(Fanny J. Crosby)

13

VARIATION ON A THEME

"And Naomi said to her two daughters-in-law, "Go, return each to her mother's house. The LORD deal kindly with you, as you have dealt with the dead and with me" (Ruth 1:8).

"Then Naomi said to her daughter-in-law, "Blessed be he of the LORD, who has not forsaken His kindness to the living and the dead!" And Naomi said to her, "This man is a relation of ours, one of our close relatives" (Ruth 2:20).

"Then he said, "Blessed are you of the LORD, my daughter! For you have shown more kindness at the end than at the beginning, in that you did not go after young men, whether poor or rich" (Ruth 3:10).

* * *

Great composers have produced famous works that were skilfully built on musical themes and have paid tribute to the original scores while showing their own mastery of them. As we read and re-read the four chapters of Ruth, we trace a theme written by a divine hand, the melody of which is taken up and expressed in a variety of ways by different individuals. Although it can be heard through Naomi, it flows more loudly from Ruth, while the echo chiefly resounds from Boaz himself. The theme is 'Grace', and we follow its harmony in the way God dealt so graciously with them.

> Grace! 'Tis a charming sound,
> Harmonious to the ear;
> Heaven with the echo shall resound,
> And all the earth shall hear.

> May grace, free grace, inspire
> Our souls with strength divine;
> May all our thoughts to God aspire,
> And grace in service shine.
> (Dr. P. Doddridge)

As we come to the end of our study, we will have exalted the God of all grace if we have highlighted how grace sometimes permits man's will when it is the servant of what He has decreed in His will. To put it briefly, all four chapters show His grace to and through each of the three main characters to foreshow:

- Through Naomi, His grace to the beleaguered remnant of Israel in a coming day;
- Through Ruth, His grace to the Gentiles through the cross;
- Through Boaz, His grace in a redeeming Saviour.

It's wonderful to see that Naomi was able to assure Ruth that *"the LORD has not forsaken His kindness"*[1] for that was a huge recovery from having falsely assured both her and Orpah that He would *"deal kindly"*[2] with them if they went back to Moab. On both occasions, she used forms of the word *chesed* that spoke of His lovingkindness, but it was only on the second that she could link it to saying, *"Blessed be he of the LORD."*[3] Could she have "blessed" him if they had gone back to their gods? Not possible! She had chosen the word *bārak*, which, apart from giving praise, reveals an attitude of heart depicted by kneeling down, as when the psalmist said, *"Oh come, let us worship and bow down; let us kneel before the LORD our Maker."*[4]

Moab had been a place of estrangement for her, just as Babylon had been for the people of Israel and as their present state of national unbelief is concerned. However, the year of His redeemed will come,[5] and they will say, *"Come, and let us return to the LORD; for He has torn, but He will heal us; He has stricken, but He will bind us up."*[6] Only then, when God proclaims *"the year of My redeemed has come,"*[7] will they discover that *"the LORD has not forsaken His kindness,"* and be able to say of Christ their Redeemer, *"Blessed be He of the LORD."*

The Grace of God Seen in Boaz by Ruth

It didn't take Ruth long to find what she wanted. She was looking for grace, and used the word *chēn*,[8] which she found in Boaz who showed it to her in ever-increasing measure. There was every likelihood that Boaz was influenced by his mother Rahab's experience of God's love for the stranger, and that Ruth came into the mainstream of this influence. The day was still a long way off from when Solomon would write, *"Let your father and mother be glad, and let her who bore you rejoice,"*[9] yet Ruth was bound to see that Boaz had learned how to treat the stranger.

Let's follow her and catch her deepening awareness of how gracious he was. It's as if God is giving us a glimpse of the most gracious Man who gives us *"grace for grace"*[10] for she found it in his ...

Presence

Having already found it in receiving his permission to keep gleaning in his field, her thoughts raced as she wondered, *"Why have I found favour [chēn] in your eyes, that you should take notice of me, since I am a foreigner?"*[11] Why was he paying any attention to a stranger? Why was he showing any regard for her? The only answer was, "Grace." It was comforting grace; it was communicating grace for she sensed it in the way he spoke; and it was undeserved grace for she wasn't one of his maidservants, yet it was inclusive grace for he made her feel included.[12]

Provision

Was he being restrictive when he set the boundary of her gleaning? No, this was the provision of grace. It was the assurance that all she needed was there. Thankfully, she understood this and didn't interpret it as being limiting. This was proved in later provision that came from his hand and from the hands of the reapers until he gave her the greatest amount of all at the end of the harvest. How carefully God was painting His picture of the One through whom we can say, *"of His fulness we have all received."*

Protection

Gleaning is backbreaking work, and Boaz knew she would tire and be thirsty. Grace anticipated this, not only by anticipating her need, but by appointing others to meet it and insisting they took no advantage of her. Grace was interested in her: not only in her being satisfied, but in being protected. This reminds that the Lord Jesus Christ is *"the Saviour of the body,"*[13] and as such is its Preserver. Like Boaz, He has ensured that we are refreshed for we *"all were made to drink of one Spirit"*[14] and, like the people of Israel, we are constantly refreshed in Christ.[15]

Promise

Naomi's earlier desire for Boaz, *"Blessed be he of the LORD,"* was echoed when he said to Ruth, *"Blessed are you of the LORD,"*[16] but he didn't stop there. Grace stilled her fears and strengthened her hope by telling her, *"do not fear"*, and assuring her, *"But if he is not willing to redeem you, then, as the LORD lives, I will redeem you."*[17] Thus she was assured by the willingness of grace. She had told him earlier, *"All that you say to me I will do,"*[18] and his reply was, *"I will do for you all that you request."*[19] This was covenanting grace and, resting on his promise, she took him at his word, *"Lie down until morning."*[20]

Principles

A man of promise needs to be principled, and Naomi knew that he was. As a man of his word, he wouldn't loosen his grip on grace or on his expressions of it. Nor would he give false impressions, so he was an example of the truthfulness of grace. He didn't hide the fact that there was a closer claimant, and he was completely honest and principled with him too. When the Lord said, *"I have given them Your word,"*[21] He was able to do it because *"truth is in Jesus"*[22] and He is *"full of grace and truth."*[23] He has nothing to offer except *"the true grace of God,"*[24] and we live by His principles.

The Grace of God Seen in Ruth by Boaz

Boaz never witnessed the faith Ruth expressed in response to God's grace, but it may have been part of what he meant by saying, *"It has been fully reported to me, all that you have done for your mother-in-law since the death of your husband, and how you have left your father and your mother and the land of your birth, and have come to a people whom you did not know before.*"[25] He never saw her fortitude when she made her pledge to Naomi at the parting of the ways with Orpah. Neither had he heard her say to Naomi, *"Please let me go,"* or to the servant, *"Please let me glean,"* but the servant let him know about her gracious ways. Her kindly caring, deciding, seeking and pleading were all witnesses of grace, and she showed the humility of grace when *"she fell on her face"*[26] before him. So he saw in her what she saw in him, and what an example this is to us who should *"be clothed with humility, for God resists the proud, but gives grace to the humble."*[27] We see it in Christ, and He should see it in us.

Having concluded our walk through Ruth's four delightful chapters, both she and Naomi are prominent from first to last. Boaz, on the other hand, is not seen in chapter 1 at all: unknown and unseen, except by God who caused the story to begin and have it written for our good. Chapter 1 is like looking at His plan to bring Jew and Gentile to Himself, while chapters 2, 3 and 4 reveal how He makes that plan unfold. There's an unseen Man, unknown in the emptiness of the human heart, and it's only by the mercy of God that our past estrangement is graciously overcome as He brings us on the journey of repentance to Himself. It's then that we make this grand discovery that He has His own Lord of the harvest for us to meet, and Redeemer to meet our need. In his own wonderful way, Boaz is an Old Testament voice saying, *"But when it pleased God, who separated me from my mother's womb and called me through His grace, to reveal His Son in me, that I might preach Him among the Gentiles."*[28]

Having said that, we also see ourselves in chapter 1, as lost strangers being led by an unseen hand from our lost-ness toward the wealth of our unknown Redeemer. We are introduced to His Bethlehemite, into whose hands God has entrusted the unique ministry of being the One who reveals and declares Him.[29] It will do us good to see ourselves in Ruth and Christ in Boaz, and, by relating all that he was to her and she to him, grow in our daily appreciation of being redeemed until we stand at His side as our Bridegroom. Safely Home, at last!

Standing somewhere in the shadows you'll find Jesus
He's the Friend who always cares and understands;
Standing somewhere in the shadows you will find Him
And you'll know Him by the nailprints in His hands.
He's the only One, yes, He's the only one,
Let Him have His way until the day is done.
When he speaks, you know, the clouds will have to go,
All because He loves you so.
(E.J. Rollings)

* * *

Through waves and clouds and storms,
He gently clears the way;
Wait thou His time, so shall this night
Soon end in joyous day.

What though thou rulest not,
Yet heav'n, and earth, and hell
Proclaim, God sitteth on the throne,
And ruleth all things well.

Leave to His sov'reign sway
To choose and to command.
So shalt thou wond'ring own His way,
How wise, how strong His hand!

Far, far above thy thought
His counsel shall appear,
When fully He the work hath wrought,
That caused thy needless fear.
(*Paul Gerhardt*)

14

LIKENESS TO CHRIST

"There was a relative of Naomi's husband, a man of great wealth, of the family of Elimelech. His name was Boaz. Now behold, Boaz came from Bethlehem, and said to the reapers, "The LORD be with you!" And they answered him, "The LORD bless you!" (Ruth 2:1,4).

* * *

Boaz shines among Old Testament individuals whose character was commendably Christlike. As we think about him, we may even decide, not only commendably but uniquely. Even so, the New Testament is silent about him, apart from being included in Matthew and Luke's genealogies of the Saviour. Hebrews 11 speaks of Rahab from a generation before him, and David from three generations after, yet, as we will discover, Boaz undoubtedly belongs to faith's unnamed legion. Scripture is far from silent about those in whom God saw Christ-likeness. Abraham rejoiced to see His day,[1] and God called him, *"My friend"*[2]; Moses esteemed *"the reproach of Christ greater riches than the treasures in Egypt,"*[3] and God called him, *"My servant"*[4]; David in the Spirit called Him 'Lord,'[5] and God said that he was *"a man after My own heart."*[6]

"My friend," "My servant," and "My own heart," but He called none of them "My Son." They bore similarities, but none of them was equal to Him. God asked a vital question in Isaiah 46:5 – *"To whom will you liken Me, and make Me equal and compare Me, that we should be alike?"* In comparison to the deities of idolatry, the answer is "No one" or "Nothing"; in comparison to true Deity, the answer is "Christ."

Paul gives the reason for this in Colossians 2:9 – *"For in Him dwells all the fulness of the Godhead bodily"* – so He is the incomparable Christ of the incomparable God. His nature is eternally unique, yet He graciously allows His servants, past and present, to share His likeness. Many did in Old Testament days, and we can in New Testament days. In the opening of his second letter, Peter assures us that *"His divine power has given to us all things that pertain to life and godliness, through the knowledge of Him who called us by glory and virtue, by which have been given to us exceedingly great and precious promises, that through these you may be partakers of the divine nature."* Presently, we can be like Him, and John assures us that, eternally, *"we shall be like Him,"*[7] but neither now nor then shall we be equal with Him. He remains incomparable!

> Lord, You are the Lamb that God provided;
> Lord, You are the Life, the Truth, the Way;
> Lord, You are the brightness of God's glory
> And no one in my life compares with You.
>
> Lord, I want to know more of Your riches;
> Lord, I want to show Your glory, too;
> Lord, I want to radiate Your beauties
> Till others say that none compares with You.
> *(A. McIlree)*

The man's name ... is Boaz

Would you have been surprised if the Book of Ruth had been called the Book of Boaz? His name is mentioned twenty-one times in English versions (twenty times in the Hebrew), while Ruth is mentioned only twelve, so we could say that her story is all about him, even though Naomi is referred to nineteen times. This seemed to be the case, even for her, for at the end of her first day's work she told Naomi, *"The man's name with whom I worked today is Boaz."*[8] Later, at the end of another day, *"she told her all that the man had done for her,"*[9] and when it came to the matter of being redeemed she was settled in knowing, *"the man will not rest until he has concluded the matter this day."*[10] It was all about him! And isn't it the same for us? We are saved through *"the gospel of Christ,"*[11] fed with *"the word of Christ,"*[12] for us to live *"is Christ,"*[13] and finally we shall be *"with Christ."*[14] Yes, it's all about the Man! But do we know what our Redeemer is really like? Ruth certainly knew what hers was like.

The Unseen

There is no mention of Boaz in chapter 1, and his absence speaks of the unseen Christ. Just as Elimelech and family had vanished from the sight of those in Bethlehem, so Boaz had vanished from theirs, yet God's eyes were fixed on him as He waited to bring him centre stage in the lives of Ruth and Naomi. As their story started to unfold, as we thought in chapter 1, they typified God's dealings with His people, Israel, who would be brought to redemption through the One who alone is the answer to the unseen Passover lamb of the barley harvest and the unseen wave sheaf that foreshadowed His death and resurrection. Through these and His glorious ascension, the One who stood in the shadows of the Old Testament took His place as the Lamb on the middle cross and as the Lamb who is in the midst of the throne that He might become centre-stage in our lives too.

A Man of Great Wealth

This is the first thing we are told about him, but Ruth had no idea of how he would share his riches or of how she would enter into them. After all, it didn't cost him much for her to glean or to gain from the un-reaped corners of the field, [15] but she knew what it meant to her as a poor stranger. The difference between her poverty and his "wealth" was found in little things, but gradually this changed until she knew the full blessing of belonging to Him. During this process, she discovered that his wealth went much deeper than material for he was a man of *chayil*, which meant strength of character and virtue. He was wealthy in his nature, in his manner, in other words a man of real substance and ability. Being rich in different ways meant that she would be enriched in different ways as she drew on all that he meant to her. In this, she pointed forward to all that we are in Christ as we draw from the riches of His goodness,[16] the riches of his glory,[17] and the riches of His grace.[18] So our Man of great wealth is greater than Boaz for, not only does He cause us to go from *"strength to strength"* – *mēchayil 'el chayil*,[19] but from *"glory to glory"*[20] and *"grace upon grace,"*[21] and these enrich our sense of belonging.

> And every virtue we possess,
> And every victory won,
> And every thought of holiness,
> Are His alone.
> *(Miss H. Auber)*

A Man of Faith

Proof of this was seen when Elimelech and family showed their unfaithfulness by leaving Bethlehem because of the famine and Boaz decided
to stay. His field was precious to him: and because it was, he depended
on it by faith as strongly as Eleazar defended his by faith in 2 Samuel
23:9,10. Just as Eleazar's sword became inseparably one in his hand,
Boaz's faith was inseparably one in his heart, and Ruth was blessed
in this as we are so much more fully in the One who is the Author and
Finisher of our faith.[22] He is its beginning and its end, its cause and its
completion, its Captain and its consummation.

Unlike Elimelech who was an example of Israel's unfaithfulness, it
would never be said of Boaz that *"Then* [he] *despised the pleasant land,
having no faith in his promise."*[23] He must have endured those years of
famine, and would have been thankful had he been able to glean what
he could and survive when the pickings were so sparse. Being faithful
in God's land, even when it wasn't yielding its pleasantness, meant
more to him than being unfaithful in Moab's land. Ruth was blessed
by his faithfulness to God and would have no reason to question his
faithfulness to her. How much more can we say this of the Man who is
in the presence of God for us! He is the ultimate faithful Servant. *"If we
are faithless, He remains faithful."*[24] He is faithful to us, having shown
Himself to be faithful to Him who appointed Him as the Apostle and
High Priest of our confession. We have no need to question our faithful
Saviour for He has already shown Himself to be the faithful Servant, the
faithful Son: Jesus, *"the same yesterday, today, and forever."*[25]

A Man of Strength

In these three chapters, there isn't the slightest indication of weakness in Boaz. Strong in faith, strong in his resolve, strong in his principles, strong in his consideration of others, strong in his protection of Ruth: he was altogether a man of strength. There was no weakness of doubt or uncertainty, of wavering, selfishness, or of poor reputation. God was his mainstay, and he was strong in Him. Outside of Ruth's four chapters we find God's evaluation of Boaz alluded to in His temple. Two pillars stood side by side. What would God call them? Moses and Aaron? Joshua and Caleb? No, He called them Jachin and Boaz[26]: combining "He shall establish" with "In him is strength."

They were good names for pillars and, although there's no indication they were named after people, they were good names for men. Boaz the man of strength was an appropriate reflection of God's choice of a pillar for he remained like a pillar in Bethlehem while Elimelech became like a log in Moab! What caused his weakness? Well, it was lack of faith. And what caused his lack of faith? Would it not have been a lack of prayer? By parallel reasoning, we conclude that Boaz was a man of strength, because he was a man of faith; and a man of faith, because he was a man of prayer. Thankfully, our Man of strength was the model Man of prayer, and still is for He *"also makes intercession for us."*[27]

A Man of Grace

There was no one like Boaz, and Ruth was impressed by his grace. She responded to him by finding grace in his eyes as the man of wealth[28]; she received from him by hearing it in his voice and finding it in his hands as the lord of the harvest[29]; she rested in him by finding grace at his feet as her redeemer[30]; and she related to him by finding grace at his side as her bridegroom.[31] She found grace that was visible, audible and tangible and, as we reach out to our gracious Saviour, we are blessed in knowing that we have all these in Him.

> Thus Wisdom's words discover
> His glory and His grace,
> The everlasting Lover
> Of our unworthy race.
> His gracious eye surveyed us
> Ere stars were seen above;
> In wisdom He has made us
> And died for us in love.
>
> *(William Cowper)*

A Man of Provision

As soon as Boaz heard that his servant had given Ruth permission to glean, he made sure that this would increase by authorising her provision. By doing this, he also made sure that there would be no thought of her going hungry. He was a true Bethlehemite, a man from the house of bread, but he could never say, *"I am the bread of life."*[32] This is the unique claim of our Man of provision: the eternal "I AM," and our lifelong feeding! Feeding is what He does; the "I AM" is who He is. And day-by-day we are finding that His garment takes shape from what is underneath.

A Man of Rest

During Naomi's unsettled years in Moab, Boaz was resting: not physically, but spiritually. In the threshing floor, he rested physically at the end of a tiring work, but inwardly he both rested and rejoiced in the satisfaction of a finished work. The Saviour was like this, too, but to an infinitely greater degree. The cross was His threshing floor, like Ornan's on Moriah in the landscape of Calvary. Physically, He was *"marred more than any man"*[33]; but spiritually, He entered into the satisfaction of completing redemption's work and saying, *"It is finished!"*[34] Having secured rest for Himself, He also secured it for everyone who hears His call, *"Come to Me, all you who labour and are heavy laden, and I will give you rest."*[35]

The Lord of the Harvest

Boaz was in no doubt as to who was the true Lord of the harvest, and all his workers knew that. There was mutual recognition of this as they responded, *"The LORD bless you,"* to his greeting, *"The LORD be with you!"* It was under his lordship that the spiritual climate of the field was set for all who gathered, gleaned, and gained. Familiar with every stage of crop management, he would have mastered an understanding of ploughing, sowing, reaping, and winnowing: identified with dirt and dust from beginning to end. He also would have a good knowledge of his seed and of his land. One evident feature of his work was that we meet him in the field, in the threshing floor, and in the gate, but never in his home until it is implied when he took Ruth to be his wife.

In Matthew 9:37 and 38, the Lord Jesus Christ told His disciples, *"The harvest truly is plentiful, but the labourers are few. Therefore pray the Lord of the harvest to send out labourers into His harvest."* As the last Adam, the Lord from heaven became the Lord of the harvest; identified with *"the man of dust"*[36] from beginning to end. In keeping with Boaz's claim that the harvest was *"my harvest,"*[37] Jesus announced a harvest that was *"His harvest,"* and, better than any, He knows the quality of the *"good soil"* and of the *"good seed."*[38] He also knows what the harvest ingathering will be. On earth, He definitely sowed with tears, but when He returns He will come again with rejoicing, bringing His sheaves with Him, in the fullest demonstration of Psalm 126:6. Boaz was a lovely example of Solomon's advice in Proverbs 24:27 – *"Prepare your outside work, make it fit for yourself in the field; and afterward build your house"* – and the Lord Jesus lovelier still!

The Faithful Witness

Ruth's introduction to the people of God was through unfaithful witnesses, but coming to Bethlehem changed all that. There she heard Boaz witness to all she had done for her mother-in-law, but it meant more to her that Naomi could testify to the closeness of his family relationship. Best of all was when he became witness to what others thought of Ruth: *"all the people of my town know that you are a virtuous woman."*[39] Did she hear rightly? Did he say she was a woman of *chayil*? Yes, he thought of her what Naomi said of him: a man of wealth – *of chayil*! So both of them were chayil-like.

When Jesus met with Nicodemus in John 3, He invited him into the inner certainty of His witness being linked with the Holy Spirit's by telling him, *"Most assuredly, I say to you, We speak what We know and testify what We have seen, and you do not receive Our witness."*[40] His faithful presentation of the gospel confirmed that what is "of God" and what is "of the Spirit" is made known only through "Our witness." Similarly, when He addressed the seven churches in The Revelation, He did so as *"the faithful witness."*[41] He neither minimised nor exaggerated what he saw. It was balanced insight for good or ill, because what He is in His Being determined how He saw them in their belonging. Seven churches heard His assessment knowing it was from *"the Amen, the Faithful and True Witness."*[42] It wouldn't go unnoticed that He witnessed to others what He thought of Antipas by calling him *"My faithful witness."*[43] If only he could say that of us all!

Redeemer

Completely unknown in chapter 1, the full purpose of Boaz remaining in Bethlehem wasn't clear until chapter 4 where he became the one who had the right to redeem. While working in the field, Ruth began to glean more than ears of barley as she observed the multi-faceted wealth of Boaz. As each of these eight features gradually dawned on her, she was brought into the heartfelt longing of one settled desire: she wanted to be redeemed. In his heart was the corresponding desire that was equally of God: he wanted to redeem, and she became his purchased possession.

From earliest days of gleaning an appreciation of Christ, God has brought us into a deeper awareness of His redemption, beginning with the dawning of our salvation *"through His blood"*[44] and ending with *"the redemption of our body"*[45] when He returns to the air for His church. With greater longing than Ruth, we wait for our Redeemer to come from a much higher gate, the gate of heaven; waiting, waiting, waiting *"until the redemption of the purchased possession, to the praise of His glory."*[46] Amen. Come, Lord Jesus!

Bridegroom

A Gentile bride for a man in his ten-fold likeness to Christ: what could be better? There is only one answer: being the bride of the Man who is Christ. Our spiritual journey began when we came in our sinfulness as strangers to the Lamb, and it will end when He takes us home in our sinlessness to be *"the bride, the wife of the Lamb."*[47] What a Saviour! Incomparable! No wonder John the Baptist made it so clear that he was not the Christ.[48] In John chapter 3, John said, *"I am not"* – *"Egō ouk eimi"*; and in chapter 4, Jesus said, *"I AM"* – *"Egō eimi."* John's faithful ministry led to proclaiming Jesus as *"the Lamb of God"*[49] and as *"the Son of God"*[50]; and to saying of Him, *"He who has the bride is the bridegroom."*[51]

We may search the Old Testament in vain for anyone with a greater range of likeness to Christ than Boaz. He was such a Christlike man of wealth, faith, grace, strength, provision and rest, lord of the harvest, faithful witness, redeemer and bridegroom; but we have Christ. Ruth was blessed through a godly man, but we are blessed through the Man who is God.

It doesn't go unnoticed that this little book began with funerals and ends with a wedding, and, as we absorb its message, our hearts are drawn to worship the God who had such a bright end in view, even when departure and death seemed to dominate the picture. In a greater way, we look at the rejection, death and burial of our Saviour and take greater note that God has a brighter prospect in view for those who know Him. The day is coming when we will hear *"as it were, the voice of a great multitude, as the sound of many waters, and as the sound of mighty thunderings, saying, "Alleluia! For the Lord God Omnipotent reigns! Let us be glad and rejoice and give Him glory, for the marriage of the Lamb has come, and His wife has made herself ready."*[52] Well might we worship: we are going to a wedding!

Jesus, I am resting, resting in the joy of what Thou art;
I am finding out the greatness of Thy loving heart.
Thou hast bid me gaze upon Thee, as Thy beauty fills my soul,
For by Thy transforming power, Thou hast made me whole.

O how great Thy loving-kindness, vaster, broader than the sea!
O how marvellous Thy goodness lavished all on me!
Yes, I rest in Thee, Beloved, know what wealth of grace is Thine,
Know Thy certainty of promise and have made it mine.

Simply trusting Thee, Lord Jesus, I behold Thee as thou art,
And Thy love, so pure, so changeless, satisfies my heart;
Satisfies its deepest longings, meets, supplies its ev'ry need,
Compasseth me round with blessings: Thine is love indeed.

Ever lift Thy face upon me as I work and wait for Thee;
Resting 'neath Thy smile, Lord Jesus, earth's dark shadows flee.
Brightness of my Father's glory, sunshine of my Father's face,
Keep me ever trusting, resting, fill me with Thy grace.

(Jean Sophia Pigott)

15

MUTUAL SUPPORT

"The Preacher sought to find acceptable words; and what was written was upright—words of truth. The words of the wise are like goads, and the words of scholars are like well-driven nails, given by one Shepherd. And further, my son, be admonished by these. Of making many books there is no end. Of making many books there is no end."[1]

Solomon warns us to expect that they will never match *"The words of the wise"* or equal their God-given purpose. But how do we tell the difference? Solomon has given us three key proofs:

* They reflect the inspired Word by being delightful and truthful. They convey divine pleasure and reflect divine truth.

* They prompt us, like *goads*, to focus on divine direction; and, like *nails*, they fix thoughts in our minds that are consistent with divine instruction and on the One who truly is our *"nail in a sure place."*[2]

* The writers may be different, from differing backgrounds and experience, but they unite under the divine guidance of *one Shepherd*.

We made a very important premise in the first paragraph of our introduction to this book: The story of Ruth has found an honoured place in literature, but, right at the outset, we salute its much more highly prized place in Scripture. The romance of literature can stand on its own, needing neither background nor foreground, and most authors would derive satisfaction if their particular book gained recognition for its individuality. The Bible is never like that. The revelation of Scripture is completely different. Unlike literature's independence, the interdependence of all scriptural content reveals that background and foreground are essential to each individual part, and that Divine authorship is satisfied by its overall harmony. Ruth's contribution beautifully reflects this. In fact, if we miss the wonder of its wider application, we miss its true relevance.

The Word of Promise

The last fourteen chapters should have proved this to us, but now, with Solomon's three points in mind, we can review the book of Ruth believing that it is well able to answer two vital questions. How does it support the rest of Scripture? And how does the rest of Scripture support it? By the leading of the Holy Spirit we can trace how God never intended that any of His writers would be independent of the others, but that each and every one would contribute to the overall harmony and authority of the canon of His Word. Two lines of thought will help us to confirm how the book of Ruth meets this divine requirement. Firstly, we may ask how it fulfils the promises of God? And then, how it complies with the prophecies of God?

God-honouring and God-honoured

Take, for example, God's promise in 1 Samuel 2:30 – *"For those who honour Me, I will honour."* Although spoken by an unnamed man of God to Eli, the principle stands true and can be applied more widely than to its immediate priestly context. Had all the kings of Israel lived by it, the kingdom would have been in better shape, but they chose to discover what the man of God went on to say, that *"those who despise Me shall be lightly esteemed."* It makes a very fitting promise for us to remember and uphold in our own lives, and a warning to avoid. Ruth certainly lived by it long before it was written, and all four chapters of her story show this very clearly. Right from the start, and way before Boaz came on the scene, she was committed to honouring God. Unlike Orpah, Ruth never caused her parents to find out that she was of the give-up-and-go-back type. It was her wonderful declaration of intent that silenced Naomi and caused her to see *"that she was stedfastly minded."*[3]

Naomi's attempted dissuasion had worked with Orpah, but not with Ruth; faith overcame the obstacles, and she focused on the course that would prove that being God-honouring would lead to being God-honoured. Naomi should have been encouraging Ruth and attracting her to Ephrathah's fruitfulness, not discouraging her. Isn't it tragic when a believer does the adversary's work by giving wrong advice and attempting to deflect someone from doing what's right?

During the Summer Olympics in 2004, Vanderlei Cordeiro de Lima of Brazil was suddenly confronted by a spectator while competing in the marathon and lost his lead for the gold medal. In a spiritual sense, Paul challenged the Galatians, *"You were running well. Who hindered you from obeying the truth?"*[4] Peter also was concerned when he warned, *"Beware lest you fall from your own stedfastness, being led away by the error of the wicked.*"[5] Ruth was tested at this very early stage and, before setting foot in Bethlehem, learned what sort of advice to resist and which to accept. It was a necessary part of learning, by the inner strengthening of the call of God, how to make stedfastness her own, and never fall from it.

Spiritually speaking, none of us can run in the strength of someone else's stedfastness. We have to make it our own, and by whatever degree we possess it, we go forward or fall back, either helped by *"the way of the upright"*[6] or hindered by *"the way of the wicked."* There is no doubt that shallow belief needs no more than the shallow reasoning of shallow opposition to make it lose ground, and even more so in these days when shallow conviction and understanding of God's Word is so prevalent. Solomon's advice still stands: *"The righteous should choose his friends carefully, for the way of the wicked leads them astray."*[7]

If Ruth was "stedfastly minded" in chapter 1, she was even more so by the time she took the initiative at the beginning of chapter 2 to *"go to the field, and glean ears of corn after him in whose sight I shall find grace."*[8] How noticeable it is that the choice of place and character of the person were her own and not Naomi's, yet she was the one who knew both! There's a real lesson here: our choices are in safe hands when they are part of being "stedfastly minded." She had heard from Naomi that the LORD had visited His people by giving them bread, and instinctively knew that her empty hands of faith could be filled only by the full hand of God's grace.

So her trust was in the LORD before she began to know that Boaz was the one through whom His full hand would fill hers. Little did she know, though shortly she would begin to discover it, that God was giving her early proof through Boaz that, *"Those who honour Me, I will honour."* So she was doubly honoured: for her own faithfulness, but always through the faithful man who began to fill her hand, her conversation, and her life. Whether by her own handfuls in gleaning, in additional handfuls from reapers in their giving or by receiving directly from the hand of Boaz himself, in every handful she held she traced his hand and the hand of their faithful God.

This was evident from the beginning of the harvest in chapter 2 to its end in chapter 3. It continued as God honoured her by honouring Boaz when he redeemed her at the gate and she became his bride in chapter 4. Overall, Ruth would have had ample opportunity to speak of *"the good hand of my God upon me."*[9] But what was the secret of Ruth's honouring and being honoured? The answer lies in another of God's great promises: *"Trust in the LORD with all your heart, and lean not on your own understanding; in all your ways acknowledge Him, and He shall direct your paths."*[10]

All Your Heart ... All Your Ways

These are the vital signs of being God-honouring. Many make a profession of committing their lives to Jesus Christ, and it has become part of the language of modern evangelism, while bearing no resemblance to New Testament definitions. Mind you, it rather demonstrates how readily easy-believism is followed by easy-discipleship. It's profession without conviction, salvation without conversion, and confession without true commitment. It may be claimed to be heartfelt, but is it life-changing? Ruth's conversion from ungodly Moab to godly Bethlehem came with her own heartfelt version of commitment, which indicated she knew it was life-giving, life-changing and lifelong.

* *"Do not urge me to leave you or turn back from following you;*

A clean break from the past – its ways, its company, and its gods – that no longer held any appeal.

* for where you go, I will go, and where you lodge, I will lodge. Your people shall be my people, and your God, my God.

This took care of the present with a real change of direction and devotion that governed her decisions.

* Where you die, I will die, and there will I be buried. Thus may the LORD do to me, and worse, if anything but death parts you and me.

This was her sense of the future – a life-changing call from God, and a lifelong call to God.

It was no flash in the pan. No, it changed her heart and her ways. More than that, the change affected "all her heart," and she became an early example of Hebrews 4:12, in that the thoughts and intentions of her heart were changed to such an extent that they shaped "all her ways." Her allegiance, diligence and obedience were above reproach, and demonstrate what Paul meant when he closed his first letter to the church in Thessalonica with this longing for them, *"Now may the God of peace Himself sanctify you completely; and may your whole spirit, soul, and body be preserved blameless at the coming of our Lord Jesus Christ."*[11]

Oh, this is the key to becoming God-honouring: it takes a work of God, not merely a work of our will. Like our salvation, our sanctification begins with Him; with the Holy one helping us to be holy. This allows Him to change what we are, before allowing Him to change what we do. It's one thing to desire Ruth's outwardly manifested triplet of changed direction, devotion and decision-making, but quite another to desire

God's inner working that sets us apart in spirit, soul, and body. If the inward is in His hands, the outward will follow. But – and it's a big but – if we attempt to have the outward triplet without the reality of the inner, we will fail.

Ruth's reputation proves this. It didn't take long for her stedfastness to close Naomi's mouth in chapter 1, nor did it take long for her to open the foreman's mouth in chapter 2. By the time we come to chapter 3:11, Boaz was in no doubt that he could voice the general opinion of her: *"all the people of my town know that you are a virtuous woman."* Initially, they saw how God-honouring she was; ultimately, they saw how God-honoured she was. What a testimony! They saw what he saw. Now then: what about us? Do we ever spend enough time seeing in each other what our Redeemer sees in us? This is not always so, is it? Sadly, right from the days of the early churches, God had to speak through James, the Lord's brother, about the damaging use of the tongue, and warn them through Paul, *"If you bite and devour one another, beware lest you be consumed by one another."*[12] As those who are saved by redeeming grace, bought with His precious blood, and bound together by Calvary's ties, we should see what our Saviour sees in us – with *all our hearts* and in *all our ways!*

The Word of Prophecy

We also noted in the introduction how closely the book of Ruth fore-shadows God's purpose for Jew and Gentile, as outlined by Paul in his letter to the Romans. This in itself gives remarkable credence to Ruth's story and helps us to recognise its meaningful place in Scripture. Far from being a fable or mere allegory, it sits comfortably among other Old Testament teaching such as the portrayal of the cross of Christ in Abraham's willingness to offer Isaac in Genesis 22, and the overall presentation of the tabernacle in Exodus, *"which is a parable for the time now present."*[13] Examples are many, including the opportunity to consider Boaz among other delightful individuals who foreshadow Christ in all the Scriptures. But there's also the collective aspect of seeing the remnant of the nation of Israel represented in Naomi, and God's purpose for Gentiles prefigured in His dealings with Ruth.

His Reward is With Him

Nestling among the many Old Testament prophecies regarding Israel's Messianic deliverance, God assured them through Isaiah 62:11, *"Say to the daughter of Zion, 'Surely your salvation is coming; behold, His reward is with Him, and His work before Him.'"* There is no doubt that Naomi was rewarded for the change of heart that brought her into the blessing of coming back to Bethlehem, and a future day will see the nation being blessed by coming to Christ. He will bring them into new covenant blessing with a complete change of heart and changed ways. What a testimony they will become to the nations when God gives "His reward," performs "His work," and fulfils His word. The process is detailed for us in Ezekiel 36:23-28:

"And I will sanctify My great name, which has been profaned among the nations, which you have profaned in their midst; and the nations shall know that I am the LORD," says the LORD GOD, "when I am hallowed in you before their eyes. For I will take you from among the nations, gather you out of all countries, and bring you into your own land. **SANCTIFICATION**

Then I will sprinkle clean water on you, and you shall be clean; I will cleanse you from all your filthiness and from all your idols. **PURIFICATION**

I will give you a new heart and put a new spirit within you; I will take the heart of stone out of your flesh and give you a heart of flesh. **CONVERSION**

I will put My Spirit within you and cause you to walk in My statutes, and you will keep My judgments and do them. Then you shall dwell in the land that I gave to your fathers; you shall be My people, and I will be your God." **COMMUNION**

Like Naomi, they will come from their places of foreign gods, turn from their disobedience to Mosaic law and submit themselves to the blessing of Messianic law, which will be written, *"not on tablets of stone but on tablets of flesh, that is, of the heart."* In this they will reflect the present-day believer's experience of 2 Corinthians 3:3, just as Hebrews 8:10 corresponds with Hebrews 10:16 with God putting His laws into renewed minds to be learned and in renewed hearts to be loved.

The Reward of the Inheritance

Among the choice things Boaz ever said to Ruth was his expressed desire on their first day of meeting: *"The LORD repay your work, and a full reward be given you by the LORD God of Israel, under whose wings you have come for refuge."*[14] What work did he mean? Was it her effort as a gleaner? No, it was for her actions as a seeker: faithfulness to her mother-in-law, forsaking her own father and mother, for leaving her homeland and coming to the people of God. But Boaz recognised the deeper motivation underlying all that: the reward wasn't simply for her doing, but for what he saw in her being. By speaking so freely to her of the revered Names of Jehovah and of Jehovah Elohim, he indicated that he already knew she had come under His wings for refuge (Heb. from *chāsāh*), which suggests fleeing to Him for protection. No god could have given this in Moab, yet she was assured that the God of Israel not only could, but would.

> Under His wings I am safely abiding;
> Though the night deepens and tempests are wild,
> Still I can trust Him, I know He will keep me;
> He has redeemed me, and I am His child.

> Under His wings—what a refuge in sorrow!
> How the heart yearningly turns to His rest!
> Often when earth has no balm for my healing,
> There I find comfort, and there I am blest.
> *(William Orcutt Cushing)*

Ruth's greatest honour came through her redeemer and in her bridal union with him, but the truth is that she was wonderfully blessed in the inheritance that meant everything to Boaz. And is it not even more so with Christ and us? Our deliverance was designed in eternity past – when God *"chose us in Him before the foundation of the world"*[15] – and designed for eternity to come. With great anticipation, we wait for His return and for Him to *"present her to Himself a glorious church"*[16] when we shall be *"before the presence of His glory with exceeding joy."*[17] The glory is all His, shared with every born-again believer through His death on the cross, through which *"It was fitting for [God], for whom are all things and by whom are all things, in bringing many sons to glory, to make the captain of their salvation perfect through sufferings."*[18]

God's purpose, in offering His Son and bringing many sons to glory, is perfectly in keeping with His nature, and means that the perfect and perfecting work is all His too. Fellow-believer, *"He who has begun a good work in you will complete it until the day of Jesus Christ."*[19] You did not bring yourself to Him for salvation. It was His work – *"This is the work of God, that you believe in Him whom He sent."*[20] Nor is the work of daily sanctification your own. It also is His – *"For it is God who works in you both to will and to do for His good pleasure."*[21]

You may say, 'But in the previous verse Paul said that we should *"work out* [our] *own salvation with fear and trembling."'* But note the preposition he used. He said we have to work "out" our salvation, which we do by the help of the Holy Spirit, and didn't say we have to work "for" it. In the true sense of working it out, we work with Paul's urging in mind: *"And whatever you do, do it heartily, as to the Lord and not to men, knowing that from the Lord you will receive the reward of the inheritance; for you serve the Lord Christ."*[22] Yes, with greater expectation than Ruth's, and according to Revelation 19:7, let us apply her story to ourselves whilst longing to hear that glorious proclamation, *"Let us be glad and rejoice and give Him glory, for the marriage of the Lamb has come, and His wife has made herself ready."*

Meanwhile, as we look for the day of eternal compensation, let us live as closely as we possibly can to the Lamb, our Redeemer. Better than Ruth, the ingathering of His harvest is coming, and so is the wedding!

> If the path I travel lead me to the cross,
> If the way Thou choosest bring me pain and loss,
> Let the compensation daily, hourly, be
> Shadowless communion, blessed Lord, with Thee.
> *(Margaret E. Barber)*

165

16

CONCLUSION

Our theme for this series, 'Men God Moved,' accepts that God was their Mover and that divine intent lay behind each writer. We also accept that, since He knows the end from the beginning,[1] He foreknew each writer and the content of the messages He would give. This also presupposes that He knew why He wanted to speak through them, and to whom. As far as the latter is concerned, the hearers would be contemporary with the writer, and God would have intended to move them. However, His revelation has wider application, as we learn from Romans 15:4 – *"For whatever things were written before were written for our learning, that we through the patience and comfort of the Scriptures might have hope."* Well might we borrow Paul's earlier comment about Abraham in Romans 4:23 and apply it to each writer: *"Now it was not written for his sake alone ... but also for us,"* and, by taking their messages to heart, discover that we also are moved.

If the closing verse of the book of Judges points us back to years of adversity for the people of God under the hand of the enemy, the opening verse of Ruth directs us forward to their years of adversity under the hand of God. Adversity is a testing ground, and in this context the story of Boaz has something preciously common with that of Job. Boaz reacted differently to it than Elimelech, and Job's trusting approach caused him to ask his doubting wife, *"Shall we indeed accept good from the hand of God, and shall we not accept adversity?"*[2] Boaz was very much of the same mind, and his godly acceptance led him to depend on the One who would cause Solomon to write, *"A friend loves at all times, and a brother is born for adversity."*[3]

Little would Boaz have thought that Ruth (from *rā'āh* – companion) would be the friend that God would bring into his life as his adversity turned to prosperity, yet this was the man who proved Solomon's words long before he wrote them: *"In the day of prosperity be joyful, but in the day of adversity consider."*[4] It was in the joy of his prosperity that he went to *"lie down at the end of the heap of grain,"*[5] and it was there that Ruth, the friend, *"lay at his feet until morning."*[6] What a glorious picture! The Lord of the harvest was entering into the joy of it, yet God had more to reveal. She was to be the bride for the bridegroom, and his adversity was crowned with prosperity.

His story, and hers, combine in such a wonderful way to depict the Lord Jesus Christ, *"who for the joy that was set before Him endured the cross."*[7] In the full anticipation of His prosperity He faced the ultimate adversity and, as the result, we bow at His feet – our present Lord of the harvest, and future Bridegroom!

Ruth's story probably stands among the most easily read, understood and enjoyed portions of God's Word, and one by which we are most easily moved. The evidence of God's grace is hall-marked in her meteoric rise from obscurity in Moab to featuring so prominently in the kingly line through which our Lord Jesus Christ was born. A barren place yielded a woman from whom David the king would come, just as the next book yielded a barren woman through whom Samuel the prophet would come. Such are the ways of God! However, Ruth's singleness of heart and prominence don't mean that we should view her in isolation, even though the divine plan elevated her from gleaning to glory. God has many great characters in His Word, men and women who stood out from the rest, yet never separated from them, for his purposes always go far beyond the individual, even when they tower above their fellows.

Gleaners must have reapers and a master. Leaders must have followers. Kings must have subjects, and bridegrooms must have brides. Moses could never function without Aaron, the prophet must have a priest, and neither could operate without a people. In the wisdom of God, it's ever the case that individuality is at its best in a community, and interdependence is designed to achieve much more than independence.

From Genesis to Malachi, the Old Testament was richly blessed with men and women through whom their generations proved that *"As for God, His way is perfect,"*[8] yet servants, prophets, priests and kings all point to a greater Man of whom we can say, "As for God, He is perfect." He verified this Himself when He said, *"I am the way"*[9] by which He combined who He is, the eternal "I AM," with what He has for us, "the way." It was from all these books that the risen Saviour spoke to the two on their way home to Emmaus, and caused their hearts to burn.[10]

If ever a book was designed to warm the heart, it's the book of Ruth, for its four chapters convey the unlikely union of a Bethlehemite and a Moabite and foreshadow the bridal bond between Christ and His church, between the Son of God from heaven and sinners on earth. With such a lofty eternal theme locked within its brevity, we thank God for moving one of His servants to write it – many authorities suggest it was Samuel – and for moving us through it. In Ruth, it kindles thoughts of ourselves;

in Boaz, it ignites thoughts of Christ. May He, like the bridegroom in the Song of Songs, put in His hand by the hole of the door, and our hearts be moved for Him.[11]

Burn in me, Fire of God,
Burn till my heart is pure;
Burn till Your life shines out in me,
Steadfast and strong and sure.

Burn in me, Fire of God,
Spare not for price nor pain;
Burn till all dross of earth consume,
Only Your gold remain.

Burn in me, Fire of God,
Burn till Your eye can see
Jesus' own image, strong and sure
Formed by Your grace in me!
(Margaret Clarkson)

FOOTNOTES

1 INTRODUCTION

(1) Rom.11:33 (2) Acts 13:22 (3) Ruth 4:22 (4) Ruth 1:13 (5) See also Isa.66:8; Jer.31:31-34; Zech.12:10 (6) Jn 4:22 (7) Prov.30:27 (8) 1 Sam.8:19 (9) Jn 19:15 (10) 1 Cor.15:57; 2 Cor.2:14; Heb.2:14; 1 Jn 3:8 (11) Ps.115:3 (12) Gen.49:10, RV (13) Hos.13:11 (14) 1 Sam.17 (15) Acts 13:22 (16) Rom.1:3 (17) Matt.1:1 (18) Job 13:7 ASV & RV (19) Eph.2:13; Col.1:13 (20) 1 Tim.3:16

2 THE TIMING

(1) Ruth 2:2 RV (2) 2 Sam.5:10 (3) Est.10:3 (4) Ezek.40:4; 43:2 (5) Ps.22:1,18; 31:5; 34:20 – see Matt.27:46; Mk.15:34; Jn 19:24; Lk.23;46; Jn 19:36 (6) Acts 2:25-35 (7) Heb.3:1 (8) Ex.18:17,18 (9) Ex.18:21 (10) Heb.9:15 (11) Heb.7:25 (12) Ex.31:10; Num.20:28 (13) Josh.2:10,11 (14) Ex.15:14,15 (15) Heb.2:14 (16) Jer.31:10-12 (17) Deut.16:16

3 THE DECISION

(1) Gen.8:22 (2) Num.18:27 (3) Eph.1:3 (4) Amos 8:11 (5) Amos 7:12,13 (6) 2 Kin.4:38 (7) 1 Kin.19:19 (8) 2 Kin.2:21 (9) 2 Kin.6:6 (10) Deut.11:14-17 (11) Ps.16:3 (12) Josh.19:15,16 (13) Gen.41:52 (14) Mic.5:2 (15) Matt.21:13; 23:38 (16) Rev.2:5; 3:16 (17) 1 Sam.28:6,16 (18) Ps.28:1 (19) Judg.16:20

(20) 2 Chron.32:31 (21) Jer.17:9 (22) Gen.29:35 (23) Ps.107:1 (24) Ps.32:5 (25) Gen.19:36,37 (26) Lev.23 (27) Rom.2:4; 2 Cor.7:9,10 (28) Ps.37:3 (29) Prov.2:21

4 THE CONSEQUENCE

(1) Gen.2:17 (2) Prov.13:15 (3) Ps.78:55-57 (4) Matt.4:4 (5) Lk.15:16,23 (6) Ps.29:10 (7) Isa.33:24 (8) Isa.1:5 (9) 1 Cor.11:30 (10) Ruth 1:3,5 (11) Is.10:22 (12) Ex.15:18 (13) Ps.10:16 (14) Lam.5:19 (15) Ruth 1:5 ESV, KJV, NIV, RV (16) Ezra 9:8 (17) Isa.37:31 (18) Rom.11:5 (19) Is.59:20; Rom.11:26,27 (20) Zech.12:10 (21) Mic.5:5 ESV (22) Ezra 9:1,2; Neh.13:23-25 (23) Jer.48:4 (24) Josh.7:21 (25) Rev.2:4

5 RETURNING TO THE LAND

(1) Job 29:13 (2) Heb.10:25 (3) Ps.84:6 (4) Ruth 2:20 (5) Gen.2:24 (6) Gen.25:8; 35:29; 49:33 (7) Num.20:24; 27:13 (8) Judg.2:10 (9) 2 Sam.12:23 (10) 1 Sam.3:17; 25:22; 2 Sam.19:13; 1 Kin.2:23 (11) 2 Sam.15:21 (12) Gal.3:24

6 WALKING TOGETHER

(1) Mic.5:2 (2) Matt.21:10 (3) Lk.1:32 (4) Ps.48:2 (5) Ps.145:3 (6) Ps.77:13; Isa.46:5 (7) Heb.2:3 (8) Tit.2:13 (9) Heb.4:14; 10:21; 13:20 (10) Lam.3;22,23 (11) Job 35:10 (12) Ps.74:16 (13) Gen.27:34 (14) Prov.14:10 (15) Ps.133:1 (16) Deut.29:18 (17) Prov.13:15 (18) Isa.13:6; Joel 1:15 (19) Ps.91:1,2 (20) Ex.23:15 (21) Judg.7:16 (22) 2 Kin.4:3 (23) Phil.4:12 (24) Gal.5:16,18,25 (25) Lk.10:1 (26) Ex.9:31,32 (27) Lev.23:10,11 (28) Prov.3:9 (29) Lev.2:1; Num.18:12; 1 Chron.21:23 (30) 1 Chron.21:23 (31) 2 Cor.10:1 (32) 2 Kin.4:42-44 (33) Jn 6:12 (34) Mk.6:34 (35) 2 Cor.8:9 (36) Judg.7:10-15 (37) Eph.2:8 (38) 1 Pet.1:8 (39) Tit.2:13 (40) 1 Jn 3:2,3 (41) 2

Cor.5:8, ESV (42) Rom.5:5 (43) Eph.1:18

7 BOAZ THE MAN OF GOD

(1) Col.3:23 ESV (2) Neh.4:6 (3) Deut.24:19 (4) Gen.22:17 (5) 2 Tim.2:19
(6) Gen.24:23 (7) 1 Sam.17:55 (8) Acts 13:22 (9) Jn 15:4 (10) Matt.13:38 (11)
Jn 15:19; 17:16; 1 Jn 4:5,6 (12) 1 Jn 2:15 (13) 1 Jn 2:16 (14) Prov.12:26 (15)
Ps.4:3 (16) 1 Pet.2:11 (17) Rom.8:13; Col.3:5 (18) Gen.17:3 (19) Ezek.1:28;
3:23 (20) Dan.8:17 (21) Jn 3:30

8 IN HIS FIELD

(1) Acts 2:23 (2) Gen.1:5,8,13,19,23,31 (3) Ex.29:43 (4) 2 Cor.5:17 (5) 1
Cor.5:7 (6) 1 Thess.5:23 (7) Prov.4:23,25,26 (8) Ps.37:23 (9) Ruth 2:19
(10) Matt.11:29 (11) Ruth 2:17 (12) 1 Thess.2:13 (13) Rom.15:32 (14) Phlm.7
(15) Eph.1:6 (16) Ruth 2:16 (17) Ruth 2:14 (18) Eph.2:5,6 (19) 1 Sam.18:23
(20) Josh.5:11

9 AT HIS FEET

(1) Lev.25:23-28; Deut.25:5-10 (2) Ruth 3:7 (3) Ex.30:17-21; Ezek.16:9;
Ps.24:3,4; 2 Cor.7:1 (4) Jn 13:10 (5) Jn 15:3 (6) 2 Sam.12:20 (7) Gen.3:21;
39:12; Ex.28:2; Eccl.9:8; S of S 4:11; Isa.61:10; Jas.1:27; Jude 23; Rev.3:4,18
(8) Isa.57:15 (9) 1 Pet.5:5 (10) Gen.33:13,14 (11) Ps.33:8 (12) Isa.38:15 RV
(13) Ex.19:8; 24:3,7 (14) Jn 17:4 (15) Heb.12:2 (16) Matt.25:21 (17) Ruth 3:9
ESV (18) Ruth 2:17 (19) 2 Sam.23:4 (20) Ruth 3:11 (21) Ruth 3:11 (22) Ruth
2:13 (23) Ruth 3:10 (24) Job 22:9 (25) Jn 1:16 (26) Eph.3:8 (27) Rev.2:25
ESV

10 UNTIL

(1) Jn 3:6 (2) Gal.5:16 ESV (3) 1 Cor.5:7 (4) Gal.4:19 (5) Phil.1:6 (6) 1 Tim.6:14, RV (7) Ruth 1:22 (8) Ruth 2:23 (9) Jer.17:9 (10) Lam.3:40 (11) Deut.28:23 (12) Deut.33:28 (13) Jn 19:4 (14) Matt.27:25 (15) Ps.76:10 (16) Job 5:26 NIV (17) 2 Cor.7:1 (18) 1 Cor.2:11 (19) Deut.25:5; Ruth 3:13 (20) 1 Tim.2:5 (21) Eph.1:14 (22) Heb.10:37 NIV (23) Heb.9:28

11 BOAZ THE BRIDEGROOM

(1) Judg.21:25; Ruth 1:1 (2) 1 Cor.5:7 (3) Lk.19:28 (4) Jn 19:17 (5) Acts 1:10 (6) Jn 10:9 (7) Job 29:7 (8) Jer.38:7 (9) 1 Sam.21:2; 2 Kin.6:8 (10) Rom.7:12,14 (11) Isa.42:21 (12) 1 Tim.1:1 (13) Eph.1:14 (14) 1 Cor.1:18 (15) Rom.8:17 (16) Ruth 4:8; 1 Sam.31:4 (17) Matt.26:67; Num.12:14 (18) Gal.2:20 (19) Gal.6:14 (20) Acts 26:18 (21) Ruth 4:7 (22) Guide Lamps for God's Lambs

12 NOT LEFT WITHOUT A REDEEMER

(1) Ex.10:23 (2) Ex.12:27 (3) Ex.12:30 (4) Jn 1:29 (5) Jn 1:4 (6) Heb.2:14 (7) Col.1:20 (8) Jn 6:67 (9) Ezra 7:28 (10) Neh.2:18 (11) Prov.10:22 (12) Ps.56:9 (13) Matt.13:4-7 (14) Num.33:50 (15) Gal.2:20 (16) Eph.5:25 (17) Gal.3:24 (18) Isa.59:20; Rom.11:26,27 (19) Heb.11:40 ESV (20) Zech.12:10 (21) Lev.23:5 (22) Lev.23:10,11 (23) Jn 17:14 (24) Mic.5:2; Matt.2:4-6 (25) Matt.9:38 (26) Gal.3:13; Rev.5:9 (27) Matt.12:18; Eph.1:6

13 VARIATION ON A THEME

(1) Ruth 2:20 (2) Ruth 1:8 (3) Ruth 2:20 (4) Ps.95:6 (5) Isa.63:4 (6) Hos.6:1 (7) Isa.63:4 (8) Ruth 2:2 KJV (9) Prov.23:25 (10) Jn 1:16 (11) Ruth 2:10 (12) Ruth 2:13 (13) Eph.5:23 (14) 1 Cor.12:13 ESV (15) Isa.12:3; 1 Cor.10:4

(16) Ruth 3:10 (17) Ruth 3:13 ESV (18) Ruth 3:5 (19) Ruth 3:11; Jn 14:14 (20) Ruth 3:13 (21) Jn 17:14 (22) Eph.4:21 (23) Jn. 1:14 (24) 1 Pet.5:12 (25) Ruth 2:11 (26) Ruth 2:10 (27) 1 Pet.5:5 (28) Gal.1:15,16 (29) Matt.11:27; Jn 1:18

14 LIKENESS TO CHRIST

(1) Jn 8:56 (2) Isa.41:8 (3) Heb.11:26 (4) Num.12:7 (5) Matt.22:43 (6) Acts 13:22 (7) 1 Jn 3:2 (8) Ruth 2:19 (9) Ruth 3:16 (10) Ruth 3:18 (11) Rom.1:16 (12) Col.3:16 (13) Phil.1:21 (14) Phil.1:23 (15) Lev.19:9 (16) Rom.2:4 (17) Rom.9:23 (18) Eph.2:7 (19) Ps.84:7 (20) 2 Cor.3:18 (21) Jn 1:16 ESV (22) Heb.12:2 (23) Ps.106:24 ESV (24) 2 Tim.2:13 (25) Heb.13:8 (26) 1 Kin.7:21 (27) Rom.8:34 (28) Ruth 2:10 RV (29) Ruth 2:13,14 RV (30) Ruth 3:7,8 (31) Ruth 4:13 (32) Jn 6:48 (33) Isa.52:14 (34) Jn 19:30 (35) Matt.11:28 (36) 1 Cor.15:48 (37) Ruth 2:21 (38) Matt.13:23,24 (39) Ruth 3:11 (40) Jn 3:11 (41) Rev.1:5 (42) Rev.3:14 (43) Rev.2:13 ESV (44) Eph.1:7 (45) Rom.8:23 (46) Eph.1:14 (47) Rev.21:9 ESV (48) Jn 1:20; 3:28 (49) Jn 1:29,36 (50) Jn 1:34 (51) Jn 3:29 (52) Rev.19:6,7

15 MUTUAL SUPPORT

(1) Eccl.12:10–12 (2) Isa.22:23 ASV (3) Ruth 1:18, RV (4) Gal.5:7 ESV (5) 2 Pet.3:17 (6) Prov.15:19 (7) Prov.12:26 (8) Ruth 2:2 KJV (9) Neh.2:8 (10) Prov.3:5,6 (11) 1 Thess.5:23 (12) Gal.5:15 (13) Heb.9:9 RV (14) Ruth 2:12 (15) Eph.1:4 (16) Eph.5:27 (17) Jude v.24 (18) Heb.2:10 (19) Phil.1:6 (20) Jn 6:29 (21) Phil.2:13 (22) Col.3:23,24

16 CONCLUSION

(1) Isa.46:10 (2) Job 2:10 (3) Prov.17:17 (4) Eccl.7:14 (5) Ruth 3:7 (6) Ruth 3:14 (7) Heb.12:2 (8) 2 Sam.22:31 (9) Jn 14:6 (10) Lk.24:32 (11) S. of S.5:4 (see RV)

ABOUT THE AUTHOR

Andy was born in Glasgow, Scotland. He came to know the Lord in 1954, and was baptized in 1958. He is married to Anna, and he lives in Kilmacolm, Scotland. They have two daughters and one son. He entered into full-time service in 1976 with the churches of God (www.churchesofgod.info). He has engaged in an itinerant ministry in western countries and has been privileged to serve the Lord in India and Myanmar (formerly Burma).

MORE BOOKS FROM ANDY MCILREE

Grace in First Peter - The Many-Splendoured Grace Shown to an Ungracious Man

As Andy says, "Tracing the grace of God in Peter's first letter is like seeing the glory of God in Romans and the greatness of God in Hebrews." In this deeply practical book, Andy takes us through each of Peter the rough fisherman's 5 chapters, and introduces us to the manifold grace of God expressed in at least 11 different aspects:

1. GRACE REQUIRED IN AN UNGRACIOUS MAN
2. GRACE RESTORED IN OUR MISTAKES
3. GRACE RECEIVED IN THE GOSPEL
4. GRACE REGARDED IN WORSHIP AND WITNESS
5. GRACE REINFORCED IN TRIALS
6. GRACE RECIPROCATED IN MARRIAGE
7. GRACE RECOGNISED IN HOLINESS
8. GRACE REVEALED IN SPIRITUAL GIFTS
9. GRACE REFLECTED IN LEADERSHIP
10. GRACE REGAINED IN BIBLICAL TRUTH
11. GRACE RE-EMPHASISED IN PAUL'S LETTERS

The Apostle Jude's Tripod - The Man, Method and Message of the New Testament's Forgotten Book (Men God Moved - Book Two)

The apostle Jude's little letter can easily be read within five minutes, yet it spans eternity past and future, history and prophecy, blessing and judgment, past revelation and fresh revelation, things known and not known, heaven's glory and hell's grief. And, like all Scripture, it has a God-given relevance for us in the present day:

* for reproof – showing when we are off track
* for correction – helping us to get back on track
* for instruction – enabling us to keep on track.

As Jude wrote his little book, it's as if he did so with the mindset of a surveyor, scanning the worrying spiritual landscape in front of him - 19 times in his short letter, Jude moves his surveyor's 'tripod' of threes to drive his point home. In addition to exploring each of these, Bible teacher Andy McIlree unpacks each verse across seven key themes of Salutation, Salvation, Contention, Condemnation, Revelation, Benediction and Doxology.

This is a very enlightening and practical study of a little understood, under-appreciated and often forgotten part of our New Testament.

The Five Solas of the Reformation

Five centuries after Luther nailed his Ninety-five Theses to the door of a Catholic church, is there still a need for reformation? Yes, the Reformers' 'Five Solas' - Scripture Alone, Christ Alone, Grace Alone, Faith Alone, the Glory of God Alone - should be engraved on all our hearts, and the need could hardly be greater for them to be nailed to the doors of today's shallow churches today that are in danger of "being destroyed for lack of knowledge" (Hosea 4:6).

ABOUT THE PUBLISHER

Hayes Press (www.hayespress.org) is a registered charity in the United Kingdom, whose primary mission is to disseminate the Word of God, mainly through literature. It is one of the largest distributors of gospel tracts and leaflets in the United Kingdom, with over 100 titles and many thousands dispatched annually. In addition to paperbacks and eBooks, Hayes Press also publishes Plus Eagles' Wings, a fun and educational Bible magazine for children, and Golden Bells, a popular daily Bible reading calendar in wall or desk formats.

If you would like to contact Hayes Press, there are a number of ways you can do so:

· By mail: c/o The Barn, Flaxlands, Royal Wootton Bassett, Wiltshire, UK SN4 8DY

· By phone: 01793 850598

· By eMail: info@hayespress.org

· via Facebook: www.facebook.com/hayespress.org

Printed in Poland
by Amazon Fulfillment
Poland Sp. z o.o., Wrocław

50129545R00105